The Prosperity Factor
for Kids

smart**investing**
@ your library®

A partnership between American Library Association
and FINRA Investor Education Foundation

ALA American Library Association   **FINRA** Investor Education FOUNDATION

FINRA is proud to support the American Library Association

Also by the author

The Woman's Guide to Money

The Prosperity Factor
for Kids

A comprehensive parent's guide to developing
positive saving, spending, and credit habits

Kelley Keehn

INSOMNIAC PRESS

Library and Archives Canada Cataloguing in Publication

Keehn, Kelley, 1975-
    The prosperity factor for kids : a comprehensive parent's guide to developing positive saving, spending and credit habits / Kelley Keehn.

ISBN 978-1-897178-42-3

1. Children--United States--Finance, Personal. 2. Saving and investment--United States. I. Title.

HG179.K4283 2007   332.0240083'0973   C2007-904512-X

The publisher gratefully acknowledges the support of the Department of Canadian Heritage through the Book Publishing Industry Development Program.

Insomniac Press, 192 Spadina Avenue, Suite 403
Toronto, Ontario, Canada, M5T 2C2
www.insomniacpress.com

Canad**ä**

Disclaimer

This book is designed to provide accurate and authoritative information on the subject of personal finances. While all of the stories and anecdotes described herein are based on true experiences, the names and situations have been altered to protect individual privacy. Neither the author nor the publisher is engaged in rendering legal, accounting, or other professional services by publishing this book. As a precaution, each individual situation should be addressed to an appropriate professional to ensure adequate evaluation and planning be applied. The author and publisher specifically disclaim any liability, loss, or risk that may be incurred as a consequence, directly or indirectly, of the use and application of any of the contents of this work.

The material in this book is intended as a general source of information only and should not be construed as offering specific tax, legal, financial, or investment advice. Every effort has been made to ensure that the material is correct at time of publication, but its accuracy or completeness cannot be guaranteed. Interest rates, market conditions, tax rulings, and other investment factors are subject to rapid change. Individuals should consult with their personal tax advisor, accountant, or legal professional before taking any action based upon the information contained in this book.

To my amazing mother, Kathleen.
You are my best friend, confidante,
and a consummate financial guide.
Thank you for always believing in my dreams and me.
I love you with all my heart.

Knowing is not enough; we must apply.
Willing is not enough; we must do.
—Johann Wolfgang von Goethe

Contents

Preface

When Johann Wolfgang von Goethe claims, "Knowing is not enough; we must apply. Willing is not enough; we must do," he assumes that we actually *know*. His sage advice can be followed on this assumption. Using these words as a basis for the teachings in this book, keep the "knowing" in mind; knowledge is certainly the key to progress. And as Goethe advises, you will apply your knowledge by doing the exercises contained herein that will benefit both you and your child.

I know you want more for your child; it's a natural inclination of a parent to desire a better life for their young. I applaud you for your interest in learning more about the foundational aspects of a healthy relationship with money, and I don't take lightly the opportunity to be your coach over the course of this book.

What This Book Is About

The Prosperity Factor for Kids is written for you, the parent. It's a guidebook for working with your child at a pace at which you know they'll best absorb the financial teachings— at a pace that you, as a parent, are comfortable teaching them this information.

I am, however, at the disadvantage of not knowing you

personally or your family situation. If I did, I would customize these pages to your unique background and circumstances. Unfortunately, my crystal ball has a few cracks in it at the moment, so I must guess, from the plethora of financial information available, what will most benefit you and your child. With many books on the market tackling the same broad subject, I hope you'll enjoy the mix between the psychologies of money and financial fundamentals you'll find here. That's what makes this book distinctly different.

There's no need to worry if your experience with investments, finance, and money management are novice or nonexistent; that's why you are reading this book. If you're a seasoned investor and have a strong background in areas of finance, the material may be familiar to you; however, I think you'll find it's presented in a distinctive child-friendly format. I suspect you're somewhere in the middle. Whatever the case, my focus on the subsequent pages is on the experiences of your child. It doesn't matter what age they are when you pick up this book. The exciting part is that they have a clean "money slate" to build on. They, unlike we adults, have not yet been filled with the problems and stresses some find that money can bring. They also don't have debts to repay or investment losses to recoup. This is your chance to set your child on firm financial footing so that they might learn from both your success and any mistakes you may have made along the way. These teachings can help them avoid the common mistakes so many individuals make.

As you work with your child, it is my aim that you benefit as well. Don't worry if you're not good with money. Picking up this book is the first step and I promise that you'll feel more confident and knowledgeable once you've completed it.

What Is the Prosperity Factor?

The Prosperity Factor is a series of tools to identify your family's relationship with money and prosperity as a whole. These tools will help you identify your key beliefs, values, and conflicts and give you new choices about how you relate to prosperity in your own life, while giving the same opportunity to your child.

I believe that there are two key elements to your child's successful future with money: 1) the nuts and bolts of financial matters and 2) psychological factors. This book deals with the fundamental financial teachings that will fortify your child with the money management tools in positive saving, spending, and credit habits necessary for an adulthood of financial ease. What you will also find within each lesson and accompanying exercises is the importance of the psychological elements of finance. As important as numbers and uncompromising money management tools are, my experience with adults reveals that how we feel about money is as central as what we know about it. My goal is to help you and your child feel good about money while understanding all that you need for the underpinnings of financial self-esteem and well-being.

I often like to compare money and finances to health. Losing weight or maintaining a healthy body is really a simple notion. In most cases, just two simple principles need to be applied: eat less, exercise more. Unfortunately, we're facing an obesity epidemic in North America. But why, if it's so simple to choose health? There are a number of emotional issues as to why someone overeats or chooses not to workout or take care of their body. One can spend the rest of their life trying to determine where their habits and body problems came from, but I believe a more elegant solution would be to fill one's life with enough positive reinforcements, exercise, and new health goals until the old issues are taken over by the new positive choices.

The awareness of knowing something needs to be done is only the first step. As Goethe implies, we may *know* that we need to eat more vegetables and do more weight training to help sculpt our bodies, but *knowing* on its own is never enough. *Doing* must follow, and that is just what you'll experience in the following pages.

The principles of health work similarly with wealth and prosperity. The simple principles of spend less than you make, always save 10% of your income, and so forth, are sound but aren't practiced by the average person. Whatever the age of your child, as you read this book, you have the opportunity to build a solid foundation for their future financial well-being. As you instill the good eating and exercise habits throughout their childhood, you'll now be equipped to do the same with their money habits.

My Hope for You and Your Family

It's my honor to be your coach as you teach your child the financial lessons contained in this book. I have tested my material with children and adults alike and have perfected much of it during my financial career. However, you and your child are unique. I want this book to change your child's life and I invite you to contact me personally should you be left with any lingering questions upon completion of this content. It's my hope that you will start, finish, and apply the information in *The Prosperity Factor for Kids* and that it will benefit you and your family immensely.

As your coach on this journey, I am a financial expert with nearly fourteen years of experience. I've had the unique opportunity to learn from the mistakes and successes of the thousands of adults I've counselled over the years. Understanding their achievements, failures, and lessons learned, along with an introspection of your own, will provide a solid foundation for your child.

As a parent in the hectic society we live in today, your job is the toughest of all. There are few manuals on how to raise children—what to teach them, when and how to instill the values you were brought up with, and how to select the values you'd like to correct. I admire the contribution of each and every parent in the world. It is not a job that I have been blessed with as yet, so my contribution at this point in life is to assist parents with what our school systems are neglecting to teach. With government budgets squeezed tighter each year and parents responsible for so much more of life's lessons, one must seek beyond our children's education for lessons in money, finance, and prosperity.

How to Use This Book

The Prosperity Factor for Kids is laid out in four sections. The first addresses children from ages two to five, the second from ages six to ten, the third from eleven to fifteen, and the last from sixteen to eighteen. The divisions of age groups are designed to build upon each other. Should you start this book with a child over the age of five, I would recommend that you still start at the beginning because there are timeless lessons in every section.

You may choose to first read this book in its entirety and then go back each year with your child and complete the prescribed exercises in each section. The choice is yours. Only you know your child, their learning style, and their ability to absorb the financial lessons in each chapter. If you find your child is precocious and you'd like to skip ahead to more advanced sections, feel free to do so. If your child needs more time in absorbing the teachings, please move slowly. There are no right or wrong lessons for your child. My segmentation is simply a guideline and, as I know, your child is anything but average. Please custom tailor the use of this guidebook to their exclusive needs.

Introduction

I was blessed to be raised by one of the most well balanced financial teachers I've had the honor of meeting: my mother. As an adult, I look back at the lessons she imparted to my two brothers and me during our childhood. As a single mother raising three children, my mom did everything she could to afford us the best life possible. Foregoing her university education to work with my father's entrepreneurial efforts, she divorced at an early age and was left with no real experience or education. She did have the strong will of a loving parent and spent the remainder of her working years perfecting her art as a waitress.

Looking back, I'm not really sure how my mom maintained our household, paid off her mortgage, and never got herself into debt, all on a single parent's salary as a server. Had I heeded her advice and followed her financial examples, I suppose I wouldn't have embarked on my journey of self-education that would ultimately lead me to write so many books on finance and the psychology of money.

There isn't a concept or exercise contained within this book that will always be true, absolute, or guaranteed regarding your child's financial success. As we age, money and our interpretation of it becomes a touchy subject; it seems more socially acceptable to discuss one's sex life than one's salary or financial struggles. How, then, do we arm the children of the future, and your child specifically, with sound financial principles to ensure a healthy relationship with money?

My mother had three children. She taught us all the same prudent principles and concepts, yet I chose to ignore much of her wisdom during my early adulthood. My one brother followed almost every teaching she set forth. I suppose some children, no matter how nurtured and schooled, will need to make their own mistakes. The best any parent can do is to set a solid foundation and know that with years of reinforcement during a child's upbringing, some (if not all) of the concepts will seep into their subconscious mind. What you do have control over is your belief in your child to do well and your expectation of them to handle their own finances.

I have just finished a cross-Canada book tour, including a number of American stops, which gave me many opportunities to listen to the feedback of thousands of individuals regarding money and the principles outlined in my last book, *The Woman's Guide to Money*. Many adults have reasons or excuses for not taking charge of their finances. I'm not suggesting for a moment that one needs to have a goal of becoming a millionaire or being aggressive with their finances. Using my health analogy, I also wouldn't suggest that someone serious about their body choose the path of a marathon runner or bodybuilder. With matters of your money and health, you must ensure your own success. You need to empower yourself and your child enough to understand which professionals to choose to make financial issues a priority for life.

You may have heard of the Pygmalion effect. Researchers Robert Rosenthal and Lenore Jacobson observed that when a teacher is told that a student is exceptional, even when they're not, the teacher's belief in that child will positively influence the results of the child's schooling. Consequently, when a teacher is told that a child has done poorly in the past—in a particular subject, for example—that belief in the child will have an adverse effect and, in a sense, is a self-fulfilling prophecy.

The effect was also seen by another study done by Jane Elliott's blue-eyed versus brown-eyed discrimination exercise. The experiement was to illustrate possible effects that racism has on different children. A classroom was divided into two groups of children based on their eye color. The first group was told that their eye color was superior; the others were told they were the inferior group. The next day, the groups were switched and the ones who were told they had the superior eye color were now told the opposite. On both days, students were given a number of tests. As you can imagine, the children who were told they were more advanced or unique scored better that day. The very next day, when they were then condemned for that eye color, their test scores dropped dramatically, and the new group that was now praised saw theirs increase dramatically.

You might extract from the Pygmalion effect that you as a parent have a great deal of control over how your expectation of your child to do well can create a positive self-fulfilling prophecy. Many young women I council and meet across the country tell me that they aren't "good with numbers" or don't have an affinity for math, which explains their unsuccessful financial lives. Sadly, my conversations with young men are starting to echo this belief. Where do such beliefs originate? Your utter will and expectation of your child to naturally have a strength for numbers and financial concepts could assist in their future success.

If you doubt your awesome power and influence over the ability to shape your child's destiny, career choice, and financial success, consider the following story. In his timeless classic *Think and Grow Rich*, Napoleon Hill tells of his son being born deaf. At the time of his writing the book, advanced hearing aids or supports of any type were yet to be designed. Hill's relentless desire to have his child hear and his expectation of it was enough for his child to hear some sounds, to help design a hearing aid prototype, and to have an otherwise normal life.

You may have also heard of the placebo effect. This assumption states that when a patient is given a sugar pill, unknown to them, their belief in the pill's ability to work is enough for their body to create a biochemical reaction to whatever physical ailment needs repairing. You might not be as familiar, however, with the nocebo effect. This hypothesis assumes the opposite of the placebo effect because it represents the ill result that can be caused by the suggestion or belief that something is virulent. It's only been since the '90s that the term *nocebo* became popular. Before then, both pleasant and harmful effects thought to be resulting from the power of suggestion were commonly referred to as being part of the placebo effect.

The issue with suggestion—whether positive, as with the case of a placebo, or negative, as with a nocebo—is that individuals, and certainly children, are affected by the prospects set out for them. When it comes to issues of health, good grades in school, or a future of financial security, your child is profoundly affected by expectations—primarily yours as a parent.

Whether your child has an aptitude for genius, financial fortune, an affinity for the arts, or none of these talents, your gentle expectations and positive reinforcement of their ability to create a successful life starts with your belief in them.

Lessons I've learned

In my career of over a decade in the financial industry,

I've had the privilege of getting to know hundreds of individuals and working closely with them on matters of finance. I've learned that people act and think strangely when it comes to their money. I've counselled clients with multi-million-dollar portfolios who lived as frugally as though they were flat broke. I've also counselled clients who seemed wealthy and financially free of worries, only to discover that not only were they penniless but they were hundreds of thousands of dollars in debt. My clients seemed to be struggling with money issues regardless of whether they had lots of it or needed much more of it. They didn't know how to spend it without guilt or how to stop spending and still feel like a success. So if just having more money isn't the answer, what is? Since I knew my clients needed more, I started advising them on what I call "foundational" financial planning, which is the basis of my last book, *The Woman's Guide to Money*.

Although *The Prosperity Factor for Kids* is laid out with concrete financial lessons contained within each section, you will also find complimentary "foundational" teachings. The prosperity-based content is intended to get to the root of any money-related issues your child might have already developed and set them on a positive path to prosperity.

Each year, many children are born with fortunes inherited from their families, but we have also read at least one major news story about how unsuccessful some of these children are (as defined by most North Americans), given their inherent blessings. Conversely, one might cite the countless examples of immigrants who came to this country without more than a few dollars and a barely functioning level of the English language only to create their own success stories. Compared to what you *give* your child, what you *teach* them is worth much more.

Two Life Stories to Avoid Living

Two of my past clients who were an impetus for studying the principles of prosperity and balance with money were two gentlemen: "Bob" and "Tim." For you to understand their impact on my research and course of study, I must give you a brief background into their lives and their net worth.

Bob is in his mid-eighties. He never married, he never had any children, and he's worth millions of dollars. The unfortunate fact about Bob is that he lives as though he's utterly impoverished. Bob's age should provide you with a clue to some important background details. He obviously felt the impact of the Great Depression; if you could see him now, you'd see that he still lives in a state of fear that one day, no matter how great today is, his wealth could all disappear.

Bob, as many millionaires do, made his money very slowly over the course of his long life. He sacrificed greatly to build what he has today and never celebrated or acknowledged his successes along the way. A life of scrimping and saving and investing wisely did afford him the title of ultra-wealthy, but merely on paper.

The main issue with Bob is, as a result of growing up during the Depression, he's held on to the scarcity consciousness that he was born into. If you witnessed him on the street, you'd fish deep into your pocket for a few coins to help him out, no matter how broke you might be. He truly goes beyond the millionaire-next-door description. He wears only used clothing—generally, articles that are torn and tattered and fit poorly. On cold winter nights, he'll double up on sweaters and socks before turning up the furnace as a last resort.

You might be questioning what is wrong with Bob. He doesn't have children or a wife to provide for after his death, why not spend a little as his family, friends, and advisors have urged him to do so that he can enjoy his life?

Moving on to the second client, Tim, who happens to be the antithesis of Bob in almost every aspect of his life. Tim is in his mid-fifties, is a professional, and has been earning nearly a million dollars net per year for almost ten years. Many find this fact impressive. If you do, read on.

Unlike Bob, Tim loves opulence and has, not one, but two very expensive luxury cars, spends time pampering himself at the spa several times a week, loves to eat out most days, and is closing his fourth divorce. Tim loves to live large. Tim's net worth, you ask? Close to three-quarters of a million dollars—in the hole. I hope you find it shocking that he's been earning nearly a million dollars a year and has almost a million dollars of debt. Tim has made many poor investment decisions over the years, and these, coupled with an ego that demands attention, have created a massive amount of debt. His goal to retire comfortably in a few years obviously won't happen.

I illustrate the stories of Bob and Tim for a few reasons. First, it's important to recognize what caused the mess both these gentlemen have created with their financial lives. In the case of Bob, he never stopped to check-in with himself and recognize when enough was enough. He failed to strike a balance between saving and spending, and as a result, his fortune has mostly amassed grief in his life.

Studying Tim, his childhood was that of a typical baby boomer until the age of sixteen when his father passed away. As the newly named man of the household, he had to support his family at a young age. He lived in a neighborhood and attended school with wealthy children, but his family always struggled to make ends meet. Giving up his childhood prematurely to support his family, he watched what others had and what he was forced to give up. Tim vowed to have everything he wanted, whenever he desired it, when he grew up. The problem with Tim is that he never really grew up. He failed to pause in his adulthood and define his worth other than in a material fashion.

The stories of Bob and Tim also influenced me (and I hope you as well) as to how I would forever define *wealth*. If you simply looked at Bob's net worth, you might assume him wealthy and financially successful. But I think you'll agree that living as if one were totally impoverished while having many millions in the bank is not a sound definition of wealth. I hope you'll also agree that consistently earning in excess of a million dollars a year only to blow every dime and delve deeper into debt isn't the ideal concept of wealth either.

So what is the meaning of prosperity, wealth, and abundance? I believe that it's an internal definition and should be discovered and refined between you and your child over time. What's true and right for me, Bob, Tim, or anyone else differs from what's right for you and your family. To be sure, Bob is a great teacher of holding onto money and amassing large quantities, unlike Tim. On the other hand, Tim enjoyed his money immensely, while Bob could barely take care of his basic needs.

Defining Wealth

While on tour for *The Woman's Guide to Money*, the media often asked if my book would make readers into millionaires. I always responded the same way: only if they want to be. Too many people lack the understanding of the continual effort and forfeit it takes to be ultra-wealthy. These people often don't take the time to investigate what is necessary to achieve such lofty financial goals and, consequently, don't realize what other parts of their lives might then fail. As the saying goes, "You can do anything, but you can't do everything." If one desires to be a multi-millionaire, for example, such a goal will require great sacrifices and, I might guess, a challenged family and social life. I don't suggest assisting anyone, including your child, on the path to becoming a millionaire, billionaire, or any other dollar figure unless it is what one wants. The key is identifying what wealth means to your family and what your child's goals are for the future. The choice is as individual as the clothes we wear and the dinner we might order at a restaurant, but realize that conscious choices should be made. Those desiring to become ultra-rich but never take the time to discover what that means and what effort is involved will feel like a failure until they learn otherwise. One needn't fail before even starting.

Comparison Shopping

There will be times when you observe, alone or with your child, others that are seemingly wealthy. For many, it's within our human nature to compare ourselves to other's successes and possibly even show signs of envy. I hope the stories of Bob and Tim will flash back across your mind so you might impart the lessons to your child.

It is of great concern to me that in today's society, it's quite impossible for us to compare ourselves to others as we might have been able to do not so long ago. Many children and teens, not to mention most adults, really don't know what another person is worth without being privy to their financial statements. One can only assume. I had the good fortune at a young age to work for a bank. Although I held the position of an investment manager, if my client had debt with the bank, their financial statement was within their file. I learned early in my adulthood that someone could seem wealthy even though their bank file states the contrary.

Think about just a century ago. If you didn't have the

money to build a house, you didn't have one. If you didn't have the money to purchase a lavish lifestyle, you had no choice but to live within your means. Today, with the advent of credit and the ease of purchasing far more than beyond our means, it will be a difficult task for you to help identify with your child who is wealthy and who has great credit. Even as the Bible teaches us not to covet that of our neighbors, how do we teach our children not to covet that which our neighbor doesn't even own?

I will attempt to provide you with the material necessary to develop healthy spending, saving, credit, and prosperity habits on the pages that follow. I hope you enjoy the journey and connect with your child in new and empowering ways.

Section I
Ages Two to Five

Chapter One
Learning about Money

Every adult has a financial story. What's yours? You may have had a perfect childhood filled with positive money memories and strong financial role models, or was it quite the opposite? Cynicism, especially in financial matters, seems to be the norm in our society. We complain about our money problems, but unless we have too much money (which I don't think is possible) and we don't know where to invest it, or we're paying too much tax on the interest earned each year, then we don't really have money problems. What we have are "lack of money" problems. I ask you to open your mind and consider the distinction between a *money problem* and a *lack of money problem*. Perhaps it's a problem of having a low income or an issue of too much debt to service. I know it might seem like simple semantics, but this is an essential lesson that you definitely want to consider when thinking of your child. It's rarely money that causes problems.

Determining Early Money Memories

Although I hold no degrees in psychology or psychiatry, I have spent time researching many schools of thought such as behaviorism, developmental psychology, and neurolinguistic programming. What I've learned is that one can identify the intrinsic patterns established in the past. We have an imprint period—a time in our life, as children and young adults, where the learned behaviors of others are impressed upon our psyche. Knowing this, we can spend years trying to determine what we've learned from our parents and other peer groups or we can solve our money problems (and others) by elegantly moving forward.

In section three, I'll briefly discuss how what we focus on expands. If I were to suggest that you take an introspective look into your past and dwell on the negative teachings of your parents, society, and other influences, you might, over time, discover the answers. The following questionnaire is limited but its goal is to bring to the surface some glaring and somewhat obvious patterns you might have adopted from your past. You don't want to remain in the past, but an oblivious attitude won't help uncover how you act today either. The intent of the focus is not to dwell on the negative but (to use an agrarian analogy) to acknowledge the weeds in your garden and pick them out as they pop up, so that they don't take over your soil. The key is to recognize past beliefs that perhaps no longer serve you, ones you have not recently been aware of and you definitely won't want to pass on to your child. Worse still, you certainly don't want to use them as a source of blame directed at your parents or anyone else. This is simply a way to potentially identify past weeds so you can pluck them out and prevent them from spreading. Let's briefly examine where you've come from so you can quickly move forward.

You'll notice a number of spots throughout this book that allow for introspection and writing. Please feel free to write directly on these pages. Use this book as a workbook and I'm sure that when you pick it up as your child ages and progresses, you'll be pleasantly surprised with how very far you both have come.

Self-Assessment Questionnaire—Where Did You Come From?

What were your earliest thoughts about money?

_____
_____
_____
_____
_____

What were your early positive memories and experiences with money?

_____
_____
_____
_____
_____

What was your first limiting or negative memory or experience with money?

_____
_____
_____
_____
_____

Did your parents have a sufficient amount of money?

_____
_____
_____
_____
_____

If your parents had money problems, what were they (e.g. not enough money, spent all of their money, were not able to spend their money, etc.)?

_____

_____

_____

_____

_____

What did you experience from your parents' money problems?

_____

_____

_____

_____

_____

What positive learning experiences did you gain from your parents regarding money and wealth?

_____

_____

_____

_____

_____

What did you learn *not* to do from your parents regarding money and wealth?

_____

_____

_____

_____

_____

During your childhood and adolescent years, did your friends and peer groups have sufficient amounts of money? How did this make you feel?

_____

_____

_____

_____

_____

During this period, what did you think of wealthy people?

_____

_____

_____

_____

_____

What did you *not* have growing up?

_____

_____

_____

_____

_____

What did your social groups teach you about money and wealth (i.e. religious groups, social clubs, etc.)?

_____

_____

_____

_____

_____

What core beliefs do you remember growing up regarding money and wealth (e.g. money is easy to earn, you only get money and ahead in life at the expense of others, etc.)?

_____

_____

_____

_____

_____

Did you have a piggy bank or secret storage place for your money? What was it? What did it look like?

_____

_____

_____

_____

_____

What did you purchase when you would empty your piggy bank?

_____

_____

_____

_____

_____

Where did you get money from when you were a child (e.g. allowance, birthday gifts, etc.)?

_____

_____

_____

_____

Did anyone ever take your money or did you ever lose money as a child? If yes, how did that make you feel?

_____

_____

_____

_____

_____

Did you ever take (steal) money from anyone as a child? If yes, how did that make you feel?

_____

_____

_____

_____

_____

In section four, which deals with teens between sixteen and eighteen, you can ask similar questions of your child. During those years, they may have developed some money issues that you can still discuss and correct. We'll also explore the importance of family money meetings in section two, where the opportunity to examine feelings and teachings about money are encouraged.

Our past is important in understanding our future and assisting our children to do the same. Inside us all is a child, teenager, a twenty-year-old, and so on. Just because we've aged, it doesn't mean that these experiences are gone and forgotten. Quite the contrary. They live somewhere beneath the surface of our conscious thought. By writing down and acknowledging where we've been, and doing so later with our older children, it's possible that the simple exercise of doing so might lead to an unimaginable epiphany. It could shed light on problems we've been unable to solve. However, we don't want to get lost in them or create a helpless story from them. The purpose of this exercise is to realize how far we've come and to realize how far we have to go.

Introspection can aid our awareness as long as we're careful to channel it positively. If we get lost in blaming our parents, others, or ourselves, we've lost the internal game. We have so much to look forward to if only we focus on our worthy goals: success, wealth, and prosperity, and determining a definition of these suitable for your unique lifestyle.

I'm reminded of a story that's been told by many and its version seems to change every time I hear it, but the lesson is still the same. As it goes, a young bride is preparing a pork roast for her husband. He's noticed that every time she has cooked him a roast, she always cuts it in half. Curious but not wanting to judge his newlywed, he asks, "Sweetheart, why do you always cut your roast in half when putting it in the oven?"

The bride thinks for a moment and replies, "I don't know. That's what my mom always did. I guess you'd have to ask her."

The next time they were having dinner at the bride's parent's house, the young man asked his mother-in-law why his wife always cuts the roast in half before cooking it. The mother quickly replied, "Oh, she gets that from me. You see, when her father and I were first married, money was tight and the only roasting pan we had was awfully small. The only way I could prepare an average-sized roast in our little pan was to cut it in half."

The moral of the story is axiomatic. Just because we've done something for a long time, or our entire existence for that matter, it doesn't make it right. As adults, we can consciously decide what we'd like to believe about cooking, money, raising children, or any other action or belief. Introspection is further necessary when teaching our children and challenging our own deep-seated beliefs and values to determine if they're worthy of passing to the next generation.

A long-time client of mine suffers from a lack of money problem in her life. She's keenly aware of her language and thoughts of scarcity and consciously focuses her energy on changing her financial situation. However, she has a deep-seated belief that money disappears before she ever has the opportunity to spend it. When discussing her early childhood memories one afternoon, she shared a story with me that identified a major moment in time that could have defined her adult troubles.

She remembered that she had a piggy bank and did enjoy money immensely as a child. Her family could be classified as middle class; they didn't have scores of money, but they never really "did without" either, as she described it. Then one day, a family member had given her $50. As a small child, this was an enormous amount of money that brought her great joy at the thought of spending it. She carefully placed the bill on her dresser and strategically planned out the candy and toys it would bring.

Weeks later, when she was finally ready to spend her money, to her shock and dismay, it had disappeared. She spent hours upon hours frantically racing through her room looking for the lost $50 bill. Where could it have gone?

After hours of searching, she gave up. With no appetite for dinner, she picked through her meal and sighed with despair. When her mother asked her what was wrong, she was fearful to tell her that she lost the money, but she whispered it to her mother as she could suffer in silence no more. In a blasé matter-of-fact tone, her mother told her that she had taken it in the morning because she was short a few dollars for her grocery shopping. Shock and anger filled the little girl.

As my client told the story to me that afternoon, the sadness and sense of loss were palatable. She had never thought of this event as an adult and pondered what lesson she learned at such an early age. Could it be possible that her money woes stemmed from this early teaching that "the money's all gone before you can even spend any of it"?

Certainly, one can't point to any particular situation in one's life and attribute absolute success or failure to such a seemingly insignificant occurrence. My client did admit, though, that she had a long-standing belief that money has never brought her pleasure, as she never seems to have enough to spend on herself. I hope her awareness of this situation has at least allowed her the opportunity to examine this early belief and choose as an adult to change it for her benefit.

The Banking Game—Ages Two to Five

The foundation of this book is based on a concept called the banking game. With a child under the age of five, it starts simply with a piggy bank, teaching your child that money is fun and the bank is theirs to control along with their spending. In section two, I outline the rules of a targeted savings account, while still keeping the piggy bank. Section three builds on the other two accounts with the addition of a long-term savings account. The last section introduces the credit account. With each account building on the others, I will outline teachings and exercises for each account that will instill positive saving, spending, and credit habits in your child. To ensure coherency, it is important to start this book from the beginning even if your child is in their teens.

The main purpose of this section is to teach your child about money while keeping it fun. At this young age, children are impressionable. They're watching how you spend and save and how you feel and express your thoughts about money. You should certainly consider some self-examining of your own beliefs and thoughts about money and heed the financial words you speak.

Think back to your own childhood and your piggy bank. What did it look like? Was it a truck, car, piggy, or kitty cat? How did you feel depositing your coins and bills into your bank? Did this activity bring you pleasure and were you the type that would empty your bank on occasion just to count your wealth?

Now also think back to what your bank had at the bottom of it. Was it a cork or plug of some type? And what did that plug imply? Its purpose was to allow you as a child to empty this bank at periodic times and purchase whatever you desired.

Consider for a moment what those specific purchases

were. For most children, spending included such items as toys, dolls, candy, and much more. This wasn't money that your parents needed for paying the mortgage. Your parents likely had no idea how much or little you had in this account and the spending was at your discretion. Money management, accumulation, and spending were fun.

I'll often lecture to large groups of older gentlemen—frequently they are curmudgeons from the financial industry who don't believe any speaker could teach them anything new. Thirty minutes into my presentation, the group's arms are usually still crossed and I've yet to get them to crack a smile as I'm building rapport with them. Yet, the minute I ask my audience if they could recall the experience of their piggy banks, the entire room melts. If it warms the heart of a seventy-two-year-old to recall his early banking days, imagine the foundation that you're laying before your two-year-old by systematically examining how to make this bank even more enjoyable.

Many schools of psychology refer to the years of a child's life under the age of eleven or so as "the imprint years." This refers to the period when children witness, learn, and model the behavior of their parents, peer groups, and society. This period will greatly determine how they perceive themselves and their belief in the future. What early childhood stories do you have that might shed some light on how you deal with money today as an adult? Consider sharing your story with a friend if you're not sure if there's a lesson or if the memory has any effect on your life. Einstein once stated, "You can never solve a problem on the level on which it was created." Many of us have money memories, positive and negative, that provide clues to what we think and feel about money matters today. I'm not suggesting that simple awareness will solve all of your financial woes; however, a brief examination of your past could answer questions you didn't know you were seeking the answers to.

A very positive early money memory of my own would explain my adult affinity to $50 bills and desire for fresh crisp bills. I can pinpoint the root of my memory to my mom and my uncle Alec. In a house with a single mom raising three kids on her own, money was tight, to say the least. Occasionally, while out running errands with my mom, we would stop by my uncle's car dealership. Since he didn't see me often, I had come to expect what would happen at the end of my visits. He would always pull out a very special $50 bill. At the time, this large sum of money was akin to winning the lottery. What was to follow in this childhood memory was my cherished time with my mother. Each evening, she would iron all of our clothes for the next day. It was a ritual of ours for me to sit on the basement stairs and blurt out the litany of successes and trials of my day. She would listen intently while ironing away.

After returning from a visit with my uncle, I would sneak downstairs and pull out my small fortune. I would heat up the iron, just like my mom taught me, and use a tremendous amount of spray starch to get my bill "fresh and crisp" as my mom did with our clothing and just like the bills she would request when cashing her cheque at the bank (back before the days of direct deposit).

With the recent passing of my uncle this year, many stood up at his funeral and told nearly identical stories of visiting him at his car dealership and the delight of receiving their $50 bill, sans the spray starch of course.

What money memories are forming in your child's life at this moment? For better or for worse, your child is witnessing many tangible and ambiguous actions. Awareness is the key, but it's only the first step. Take the time to examine your own first money experiences. This will ensure that you will offer your child all the options and not just teaching them what you were taught.

The Currency Game

Take time to teach a history lesson in money. Each bill and coin features leaders, landmarks, and symbols of the past as well as so many other lessons. See section three for a complete history of money for older children, but for now, pointing out such things as pyramids on a $1 bill or the various images on state quarters provides hours of educational amusement.

You might even be surprised by what your child discovers that never registered with your adult awareness. I recently attended my thirteen-year-old niece Jocelyn's band recital. Her brother, Adam, who was ten at the time, was doing his very best to stay still and behave, but during the second hour, his boredom was growing immensely. Just returning from my American book tour, I still had an American $5 and $1 bill in my wallet. I gave each to him and was delighted at his curiosity and interest in them. He carefully examined each president and graphic on the bills.

Over a half hour later, Adam was still looking for hidden treasures. He was holding the $5 bill up to the light and was delighted to find a faint but noticeable head of a man that could only be seen when illuminated. I had looked at the bill for quite some time, and as an adult with little curiosity any more about money, I would have never found the camouflaged image.

Since witnessing the delight of my young nephew, I too have found great amusement in being more curious about currency. Recently, I had two very crisp and fresh $50 Canadian bills sitting on my counter. I hadn't seen one for years.

I love the color of our $50 bills and just left them sitting there for a few days. After about day three, I finally picked one up to look at it because there are so many interesting pictures on the back that I had never noticed. If you haven't seen a $50 Canadian bill, I highly encourage you to locate one if you can and share the interesting history lesson outlined on the back of the bill with your child.

On the bill is a small picture of a book that caught my eye. I just about needed a magnifying glass to read it, but if you squint enough, you'll see an inscription that states, "Universal Declaration of Human Rights (1948). All human beings are born free and equal in dignity and rights." The accompanying picture depicts Nellie McClung holding a newspaper with the headline, "Women are Persons…" And just returning from my first visit to our nation's capital, I had the chance to see in person the Peace Tower, which is depicted on the front of the bill. As a hurried adult and with the few occasions I actually use cash for purchases, I certainly have never taken the opportunity to afford myself a brief history lesson unveiled within our currency. What a unique experience for you and your child as an introduction to both finance and the history of our country.

Foreign Money

Introducing foreign money to children aged three to five can be enjoyable, will provide hours of discovery, and will expand a mindset of curiosity. For added benefit, consider bringing out a globe or atlas to show your child the country where this currency is from.

This needn't be an expensive exercise. It can include a few coins and bills of low denominations. Consider exotic currencies such as Indonesian rupiahs or Mexican pesos. As I write this text, for one U.S. dollar, you'll receive nearly

9,500 rupiahs and 11 pesos. These foreign currencies are fun for both adults and children. You'll both feel more rich and prosperous during playtime for only a few dollars. You can find many currencies at a currency exchange house and most major currencies at your local bank. You might not be able to locate the extraordinary such as rupiahs, but perhaps the next time a friend or associate is traveling to Indonesia, you could request they bring you back a few dollars worth of bills and coins. Teaching your child to count with other currencies will ensure math time is more enriching, comprehensible, and, of course, fun!

Finding Money

When was the last time you found money? Many of us would probably need to ask ourselves when we last looked for money consciously. Did you find money when you were a child? When I was young, my mom would take me and my brother David on shopping trips. To keep us entertained, she would remind us of a game to play. So as to distract us from arguing I suppose, she'd challenge the both of us to carefully look around the store floors and keep a look out for coins and even bills. It worked every time: we would both be quietly amused and we would find money without fail. Our hunt usually produced such modest treasures as a few pennies, but sometimes they produced as much as a $100 bill.

Fast-forwarding to adulthood, I rarely find money. Then again, I'm not exactly looking for it. I have made a concerted effort to do so in recent years and seem to find a penny or two here and there and generally it seems to be covered with snow or mud. In times past, when money and I were not as good friends, I would spot a dirty coin or bill and rush past it for someone else to pick up and clean for their own. In his audio program, *Manifest Your Destiny*, Dr. Wayne Dyer shares a story about all the money he has found over a twenty-year period and all over the world, mostly during his morning jog. He places his found treasures in a clear jar and keeps them in his office as a daily reminder of our abundant universe and that when you're looking for something, you just might find it. Respecting and appreciating found money as an adult is an important life exercise and one worth displaying to your child.

Prosperity Pause

As your child starts to play and touch money, your parental inclination will be to make comments about such handling. Dealing with this age group, your child will no doubt be tempted to put a coin or dollar bill in their mouth. Knowing the germs that linger on money from countless handling, a stern scolding of, "Don't put that in your mouth, it's dirty," is likely if you haven't said this a dozen times already. Words, and the way we use them, form an integral part of the path we take towards changing our beliefs about wealth and prosperity. Every time we make a statement, we are affecting our nervous system and, possibly, exposing ourselves to thought viruses.

Like the insidious hidden cold or flu virus, consider the subtle yet menacing effects of the collective consciousness of a society's negative thoughts, or "thought viruses." These accepted notions are never questioned as they lurk beneath our consciousness. Listen carefully to friends, family, the television, and the radio and you'll find a vocabulary error that's swept the nation in the form of "anyways." Grammatically, *anyway* is the correct word, not the plural form of it. Yet, educated journalists and professionals consistently misuse this word. Have you considered that the "cold and flu season" advertised by the drug industry could in part be a self-fulfilling prophecy? That since we're told by advertisers all fall and winter, just about on a daily basis, that we will get a cold and flu this year, by focusing on these messages we increase our chances of illness?

Regarding the profound effect that words have on our subconscious regarding money and the statements that might be below your conscious radar increasing your chances of re-pelling wealth, consider how many times you've heard or said the following sentences:

- John is *filthy* rich.
- Margaret is *disgustingly* wealthy; the way she spends so freely just *makes me sick*.
- Thanks for the invitation to the mountains this week-end, but it's just *too rich for my blood*.

Can you think of a few more? Take a moment to list three or more dis-empowering beliefs and statements about money and wealth that could limit your congruency with achieving more of it:

1. _____
2. _____
3. _____

Little ears are listening and learning. How you speak about money is being heard by your child. Let's take the first sentence about John being "filthy rich." Have you heard this one before? We sometimes describe money, or someone who has money, as filthy. Let's pretend that you've just identified that you would like to be wealthy and prosperous according to your own perceptions. What's being said in the statement about John? Basically, that it's filthy to be rich. If you're guilty of making such statements from time to time, you've been commanding your nervous system to believe, not consciously, but at some level, that money is equivalent to filth. Who would want to be considered filthy or dirty or wrong? We'll just stay poor, broke, or at our less-than-ideal state so as not to create a wrong situation. How will you ever become wealthy if you think it's wrong?

If you're unable to foster a positive view of wealthy people now, especially if you're not rich, then one might surmise that you don't want to be rich one day. The same is true if you think all rich people are evil or malicious or have given up something good for financial gain. On the other hand, if you really wanted to be rich and thought it would be a good state to achieve, you would embrace the notion of supporting your future (rich) self.

I hope I've made my case and you're able to see that there might be some internal conflict when you make a statement that would appear to be as innocent as saying, "John is filthy rich," or some other derogatory comment about wealth and money. How can you not support wealth in others when this is the direction in which your aspirations are heading? It's really as simple as knowing you have a choice—a choice to decide quickly and easily to speak and think only those words and sentences that support the image you'd like to create one day, even if that day seems far away. It's always easy to take the low road, to rationalize why some have done well for themselves while you're still perhaps several or many steps away from your goal. But taking the low road in this instance, through verbal or mental bashing, has far-reaching effects beyond the obvious integrity issues. You're actually sending commands to your nervous system.

When you have your early discussions with your child

about money (e.g. don't put it in your mouth and wash your hands afterwards), consider a distinction that makes all the difference. The money itself is not dirty, but the paper and metal material has made its rounds unlike anything else in the world. You might use the example of fruits and vegetables as being good for us but needing to be washed before we can eat them. You could explain that since it isn't practical to wash money, the bills and coins don't belong in our mouths. It will only take a few minutes more to explain this process to your child as opposed to scaring them into an early belief that money is filthy.

Spending Money

Most of us love and cherish Saturday mornings. I too adore the first day of the weekend, even though I've generally worked Saturdays and have irregular hours. I would often spend most of my week thinking and planning how to best savor this day and what shopping and small luxuries (such as a latte and a few minutes of reading the paper) I would partake in.

One day, the love of my life, Wyatt, questioned my weekly Saturday rituals. Why that day? he wondered. Why can't you go shopping Thursday night or Sunday afternoon? The answer was simple for me, but I had never thought out why that was my "spending day." It was the special time my mom and I shared growing up. Since she had a gruelling work schedule (while raising three kids on her own), Saturday afternoon was the only time she had available in her hectic life to purchase the upcoming week's groceries and run errands. She always made it a "date" for us, even though it was a necessity for her. Reflecting back as Wyatt asked about this ritual I continued into my thirties, I became aware of the valuable tradition my mom had created for me and the positive association I still have with spending money on Saturdays.

Set a special "spending date" with your child as well. It doesn't necessarily need to be a weekly activity or even a weekend. Discuss your spending date with them in advance so they can look forward and link positive associations to this activity. It's important that you instill effective saving habits in your child's life and teach them about currency and finance, but it's equally essential for them to focus on later enjoying and spending their money.

Gift Giving

I don't know what your current life situation is at the moment. I can only hope that as you read these pages, you are overflowing with cash reserves and have a burgeoning income. If you're anything like the average person, however, this is not likely the case.

It's been said by many that if you can't give when it's difficult, you won't give when it's easy. I suggest that you make giving—of your time, money, and resources—a regular exercise and get your child involved every year of their life. Giving gifts to others will teach your child that there is an abundance of "stuff" in our world and will instill the all-important lesson that there are always others in need. A selfless act of love via gifting might be small but it can change the recipient's life forever. It's what reminds us of how we're all sharing this blue planet together and why the excess resources we've received in life ought to be shared.

A friend of mine recently shared a story of gifting that bears repeating. A father picked up his son from a birthday party and someone had given his son dozens of balloons. At five years old, this bunch of balloons was more than the little boy needed for his joy and benefit. As my friend tells it, the father asked the boy how they could make that joyous experience even more expansive and full of lasting memories. They agreed to drive over to a nearby senior's home. Father and son together gave a gift of a red balloon to each resident on the fourth floor. The cost was nothing and the time brief, but the memories and the love extended to the seniors were bountiful.

What simple acts of kindness, love, and generosity can you and your child extend to others? We'll discuss random acts of kindness more in section two. It's never too late in life to experience the joy of gift giving in any way and never to early for your child to witness its universal power.

Prosperity Recap

At the end of each section of this book, you will find a brief summary of what you've learned along with a number of action steps to be completed immediately for maximum effect while the concepts and notions are still fresh. Statistically, those that purchase a book rarely make it past chapter two. Please stay with me on your journey to prosperity and for the sake of your child's financial future, not just by reading on, but by retraining your own subconscious and setting the stage for your child in solidifying a positive future with money.

As you read the subsequent chapters, you will likely find that you're one of two types of people (or a combination of both): a "knower" or a "doer." Some readers just want to know more, and that's fine. I can't force you to try the exercises within these pages yourself or with your child. Nor can I guarantee that your child will wish to try each and every exercise either. My publisher and I have both benefited by your purchasing this book and I would like you and your child to have the benefit of a full, prosperous, and meaningful life. If you would prefer to read the entire book first and then come back to the exercises, they'll be waiting for you when you're ready.

You'll also see a wrap-up checklist at the very end of the book that you can check off each year as you and your child complete the prescribed teachings and action steps.

Continue to write in this book as space allows and use it as a financial journal of sorts as your child moves forward on their path to financial success. You might need a couple of extra notepads to go along with other action steps in the forthcoming sections or splurge and purchase a few memento-type journals.

Your Child's Prosperity Action Steps

- Please take the time to complete the self-assessment questionnaire if you haven't already. Did you reveal any "lack of money" issues that you hadn't thought of before?

- What positive money memories can you now develop with your child?

- Purchase a piggy bank for your child if you haven't already. Feel free to be resourceful and locate one from a garage sale or dollar store.

- What foreign currencies have you and your child explored? Have you discovered any hidden messages or meanings within the various U.S. bills and/or other currencies?

- What words have you identified regarding money and wealth that you will no longer use?

- Have you formalized a regular spending date with your child even if it's only once a month? Does your child have a schedule of upcoming spending dates to look forward to?

- Have you thought of any excess in your lives that you and your child could give to others as in the story of the balloons in the retirement home?

Section II

Ages Six to Ten

Chapter Two
Motivation and Earning an Income

The Banking Game—Ages Six to Ten

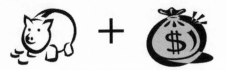

As you and your child work through each version of the banking game, I recommend that you keep their piggy bank and each new "bank" introduced in each section as they build into a money management system.

Even adults need to have fun with money. I've taught people to have fun with piggy banks even in their sixties and seventies. No age group is too mature to have a fun account where the spending has no goals or restrictions and the sole purpose is to experience pleasure with these funds.

Introducing the Targeted Savings Account

The purpose of the targeted savings account is to teach your child to save up for desired expenditures in the near future. Such expenditures might include a swim pass for the summer months or a ski lift pass for winter.

The first exercise is to sit down with your child and discuss expenditures that you are both willing to save for—in the next three months, for example. Keep this account and the goals short term, not exceeding twelve months. Find a small scribbler and write down the goals. List all that they desire and then decide together which items take priority.

Next, list the cost of each expenditure and discuss how these purchases will be funded. This is an ideal opportunity for prioritizing expenses with your child and empowering them to pick items that fit into your spending budget or having them come up with creative income solutions with you.

To chart your child's progress, have them create a "goal thermometer" either with paper or on a computer. Start with placing $0 on the bottom and the dollar goal at the top. Create lines in between that can be filled in showing how close your child is to their financial goal. Visuals are a constant reminder that helps keep the goal real. You want your child to understand that they're doing more than just saving money; there are many benefits to what they're saving the money for.

As an illustrative example, see young Jennifer's goal of saving for a ski pass as the focus of her short-term savings account. Jennifer and her parents have identified that she will need $225 to reach her goal in the next ten months. Her parents have agreed to match her dollar for dollar and will fulfill that agreement when she succeeds in saving her targeted amount. As a side note, I think it's a good idea to present your matching dollars, should you choose to do so, after your child has reached their goal and not during the process. It is a reward that should be presented to your child after their successful completion of saving the necessary funds.

Jennifer's Targeted Savings Account
SKI PASS
BY December 2008
(Now January 2008)
Goal: $225

Dec — success achieved! Thanks to Mom & Dad's portion

Nov — **$112.50** should be saved

Sept — **$90.00** should be saved

July — **$67.50** should be saved

May — **$45.00** should be saved

March — **$22.50** should be saved

- Focus on Saving $112.50 **in the next 10 months**
- Focus on Saving $11.25 **per month**
- Focus on Saving $0.40 **per day**
- Mom & Dad agreed to match savings to a maximum of $112.50

The thermometer provides a useful visual for Jennifer and her parents to track her progress and reward successes along the way. It also breaks down the seemingly overwhelming target amount into manageable chunks. Businesses know that scaling down a loan payment to just dollars a day entices buyers much more than stating the cost per month or year. Consider doing the same with your child's goal.

• Start with the amount that needs to be saved ($250)
• Identify the dollar-matching ratio offered by parents or grandparents ($1:$1)
• Calculate the net dollar amount your child needs to save ($112.50)
• Determine a time allotment for saving for the target amount (10 months)
• Calculate the monthly savings needed to meet the goal ($11.25 per month)
• Calculate the daily savings needed to meet the goal ($0.40 per day).

Next, chart their progress and create a goal board in their room or perhaps on the kitchen fridge. Decorate the thermometer with pictures of skiing and your child with their friends. Color the picture with markers or keep gold stars handy as they reach each monthly target. For a thermometer in a large printable format, please visit www.theprosperity factor.com for a blank copy.

Positive Saving and Spending Lessons

Suppose in September that you and your child have agreed on obtaining a ski pass for use during Christmas vacation. The pass is $250 and perhaps you intended on paying for this anyway. I would encourage you to elicit your child's

cooperation and creativity to help pay for this instead of paying for it all yourself. This will help them appreciate the effort needed to pay for things they enjoy and help them
understand the value of money.

Now, determine how your child will pay for this expenditure. Look at all income sources they receive such as their
allowance and any upcoming gifts (birthday, cash from
grandparents for Christmas, etc.). If you know that your child
will not be able to save entirely for the upcoming ski trip, you
might agree to match your child dollar for dollar (or two to
one, etc.).

If a shortfall exists for your child, this provides an excellent opportunity for you both to discuss other means for increasing their income to reach their goal. You could increase
their allowance for any chores they do above and beyond
their weekly duties (e.g. cutting the grass or shovelling side-
walks). Children in this age group are too young to work
legally, but perhaps you could assist them with creating a list
of income-generating activities that are close to home. Could
they enlist the help of their friends in running a lemonade
stand? What about a leaf-raking service in the fall for neighbors in your area? Your child's creativity might surprise you
as to what ideas they'll come up with when they have a clear
vision of what they're saving for.

The goal of the targeted savings account is to help your
child understand that some items and services need to be
saved for in advance. As an adult, we might need to purchase
a new fridge and stove or furniture for our home. It's not a
long-term commitment such as saving for our retirement, but
it's certainly an expenditure that requires advance goals of
allocating the necessary funds to avoid purchasing the items
on credit.

Dividing Your Child's Income Between Two Accounts

In your goal book, after you and your child have listed all expected and anticipated income, determine a percentage split between the piggy bank and targeted savings account. The split should be decided between the both of you. It can be 50/50 or whatever amount you think appropriate. I would recommend that at least 20% be always allocated to the piggy bank. As you empower your child with more financial responsibility, it becomes even more essential that they have a pot of money that is just for them—for their pleasure and without rules or responsibilities.

Sample Account Split

Income received this month:

Birthday money from Grandma	$25.00
Net profit from lemonade stand	$4.25
Allowance	$10.00
Found while shopping	$3.25
Bonus for extra house cleaning	$2.00
Total income:	**$44.50**

Split between accounts:
40% to the Piggy Bank = $17.80
60% to the Targeted Savings Account = $26.70

Even though at the age of five or six your child may be a little young to fully grasp the concept of fractions and percentages, you may wish to start with a 50/50 split each month and have your child help you figure out the dollar amount for each account. Increase the complexity of the percentage split as your child's math skills increase. This exercise will provide them with a real-world understanding of calculations that may seem nebulous while learning in class.

Setting Up the Targeted Savings Account

This account could be your child's first formal bank account. However, since the sums are likely to be small and withdrawn regularly, I suggest that it's simply a separate account at home. It could be a jar, box, envelope system, or simply another piggy bank with a label on it.

If you decide to set-up your child's targeted savings account as their first formal bank account, there are a few things you should consider. The point of this banking game and its process is to include your child each and every step of the way. With today's hectic lifestyles, it won't be possible to take your child to the bank to deposit their funds every time new dollars have built up or when it's time for a withdrawal. Consider setting something up at home to act as a holding account until you have the time to make deposits. If it's time to purchase that swim or ski pass and you don't have time to go to the bank, have your child write you an IOU and paste it within their bank passbook. This exercise is not simply to create more work for you; it encourages good saving and spending habits in children by demonstrating one of many ways to keep track of finances.

The act of going to a bank and standing within its walls can be an intimidating process. For many people, a bank represents a parental authority figure that dishes out money if we're "good" and denies us credit if we're "bad." When setting up a bank account for your child, take them with you and explain the process of a bank's operations as any other business. It's comprised of bricks and mortar and people earning a living, helping the company turn a profit that is then returned to those who invested in it.

Once the account has been opened and the ink has dried

on the passbook, take a few moments when you get home to celebrate the account balance with your child. In today's ATM-friendly environment, you can even update the passbook regularly during non-banking hours and will find plenty of blank books near the envelopes at most ATM centres. For each new goal set for this account, have your child write it on the front of the passbook. Encourage them to think about what this money will be used for and how much enjoyment it will bring them. Have them decorate the passbook with stickers and drawings as they'd like. When a goal has been achieved, have your child use a felt marker to place a big check mark on the front of the passbook. The addition of a gold star is even better. When a new goal is decided upon between each of you, file away the old successful passbook and get a new one from your bank or ATM centre. Start the process all over again.

Interaction keeps banking tangible for children. Even as adults, it's easy to forget why you're saving money at all. Having focused on goals and interacted with stickers and small rewards, saving and goal setting remain pleasurable and attainable.

Your Child's Motivational Styles

As with adults, your child may have difficulty saving for the future. There may be times when they just want to spend all the savings on an impulse, deviating from the targeted savings account and financial goals that were set. So how do parents assist in keeping their child or even themselves on track? Let's consider two basic motivational styles. I borrow these from neurolinguistic programming (NLP), and although I'm far from an expert, a brief understanding assists us all in keeping our eyes on our goals.

There are two basic styles that motivate our children (and

us too, for that matter). One might have more emphasis than the other, and understanding both styles will increase the chances for success. The first style is called "away from" and the second is "towards."

Style #1: Away From

This motivational strategy has fear or a lack conscious-ness as its basis. Life coach and motivational speaker Tony Robbins suggests that human beings have only two reasons for doing anything: to avoid pain or to gain pleasure. When using the "away from" strategy, you might focus your child's attention on the pain that they will feel in missing out on the financial goal that they have set for their targeted account. Using your child's financial account as an example, this strat-egy can be used to entice your child to do almost anything from practicing their piano lessons to finishing their home-work early after a long week.

Let's assume that you and your child have agreed to save for three months for a swim pass. It's March and the purchase needs to be paid in June. In April, your child insists he must have a new video game that's just been released and is doing his best to persuade you with his sales acumen. He proclaims that all of his friends have it already and he really needs it now! With the "away from" strategy, you would gently re-mind him of the wonderful summer that he had last year en-joying the pool all summer vacation with his friends. He wouldn't want to be left out of that just to acquire this new game, would he? The basic strategy is to create a compelling case for the pain that he will feel if he doesn't reach this goal.

Style #2: Towards

With this form of persuasion, the focus is kept on what your child will get from achieving his goal. Your attention might be on how happy he will be with the freedom to visit the community pool as often as he likes without worrying about the cost. If he's focused on his young muscles, you might point to how strong and fit his body will be by the end of the summer.

These two motivational styles can work with almost any goal you wish for your child. Keep in mind that many of us need both motivational nudges at times and it also depends on the goal. Consider an adult wanting to lose weight. Let's for a moment assume that you desire to shed a few pounds. What would motivate you more, taping a picture of a magazine model with a perfect body to your bathroom mirror, or would thinking about how this extra weight could be contributing to your ailing health, potentially increasing the chances of diabetes, high blood pressure, and worse? Perhaps a combination might be best. Keep in mind that the style could change based on the desired outcome.

Money As a Medium

During these early years, it may be a difficult task to teach your child that money is simply a medium. And to dispel the myth that tends to reside in young minds that money grows on trees, try this fun yet simple exercise.

Here's a typical summer scenario: there's a faint ringing of music in the air. Is it the neighbor's radio belting out childhood nursery rhymes? No, it's the dreaded ice-cream truck and it's heading up your street. One can almost hear the cries of young children from blocks around. Your child summons desperate calls for dollars and change. You approve this impulse buy and ask them to go to their piggy bank to fetch a few loonies for ice cream. They know it's empty. They ask you for the money instead as theirs is all gone. This situation provides a wonderful opportunity for a lesson in "exchange." You might offer the money in exchange for help in pulling the weeds for a few moments once they have finished their coveted ice-cream bar. Your child agrees and flies out the door.

Later, once your child's sugar rush has passed and you're both pulling weeds from the garden, discuss what just occurred earlier. Describe that money is used as a medium of exchange that's universal for what the other party wants. Your child could have run out the door with a household item that the driver might have taken in exchange for payment; however, our currency is a stable and guaranteed form of exchange for what we desire. Further explain that since they had used up the money from their piggy bank, they needed to create a way to earn more money.

Should every dollar your child needs require a lesson from you? Absolutely not. The above example and the many fun lessons to follow in this book are for you to pick and choose at appropriate times. If the ice-cream truck had arrived just as your hands were full taking out the garbage or cleaning the evening dishes, you likely won't have the time to negotiate with your child for something so small. However, as you read these exercises and stories, you'll know when the time is right to present each lesson in your child's life. As with any teaching, repetition is key along with an element of enjoyment. These lessons need not be complex or require rigid planning in advance. When the opportunities present themselves—at the grocery store or during a purchase at an amusement park, for example—if you find a few minutes to explain what you're doing with money and why, it will provide real-life examples that your child can comprehend.

Should You Pay Your Child an Allowance?

I suggest that you pay your child an allowance, but with a few caveats. First, you may want to consider "paying" your child for work as discussed earlier in this section. An excellent early lesson for your child is the lesson of reciprocity. They won't be given allowance money as an adult, but the work need not be too intensive for a monthly allowance either. Assisting with dinner dishes in the evening, vacuuming on weekends, or whatever household duties you feel that they can handle would be acceptable.

Second, increase their allowance with increased responsibility as opposed to just age. If you have a seven- and ten-year-old, for example, should they be paid the same amount simply in the name of fairness? Their allowances should reflect their duties. If you have a precocious young seven-year-old who is willing to "do more" than your ten-year-old for increased remuneration, that's healthy. It would then be up to your ten-year-old to choose to increase their duties as well or their allowance would remain the same.

Last, the most important part of being paid an allowance is that it gives some control to your child over their spending and saving decisions. You might ask why you need to consider this at all—as a parent, you take care of your child and provide them with everything they need and more. You likely also succumb to many if not every want they have—many parents do. During my childhood, my mom never paid us an allowance. There certainly isn't a right or wrong answer here, but consider this: if you were going to purchase a number of luxury items for your child in a given year anyway, you might consider giving those decisions to your child to play with in the banking game or otherwise. You might be pleasantly surprised that your child's wants decrease as they now have to make the decision of what *they* want to buy. Instead of the wish list increasing every time you are asked for something, it's up to them to decide if they want to now spend "their money" on the item as opposed to yours.

Remuneration for Household Chores

You may have a clear schedule of chores within your daily and weekly regimen, a portion of which your child is responsible. If you do, know that this is a reasonable thing to ask of any child, whether it's simply cleaning up their toys after a long day of play or encouraging more advanced duties for older children, such as sweeping the floor or helping with the garbage. During the early years of your child's life, it would be good to have a discussion regarding the importance and expectation of their household support.

Should your child wish to purchase or have you purchase for them a big-ticket item such as a new PlayStation or a giant trampoline for the backyard, consider assigning extra chores as work or exchange for what's on their wish list. Perhaps the task of empting the dishwasher each night—and without complaint or requiring reminders—for a time period of three months could justify the child's purchase. If you intended on buying the PlayStation or trampoline anyway, you might ask reciprocity from your child for this reward. A timeless saying that I'm sure you heard from your parents and one that I recall from mine works well here: "Don't you know that money doesn't grow on trees?" If you haven't already, why not teach your child that goods and services are obtained when prefaced with some cause, such as work or other efforts.

Using Money As a Punishment or Reward

After nearly fourteen years as a financial professional who observed thousands of adults with self-esteem issues regarding money, I would recommend that money not be used as a punishment or reward attributed to certain behaviors. Fighting with a sibling or misbehaving should be punished according to your current discipline guidelines. Similarly, good behavior such as getting along with a sibling while shopping or playing quietly should not be rewarded with money but instead with simple positive reinforcement. I don't claim to be an expert at child behavior or reward and punishment systems; I merely have seen the deep-seated issues that adults harbor, which could have been developed during their childhood.

Conversely, consider reward and punishment with money surrounding work-related issues. If your child's allowance is contingent upon certain household tasks being completed without being asked, an acceptable disciplinary action for needing to remind them might be to reduce the dollar amount paid. Equally, an increase in allowance might be offered for their overachieving or going out of their way to do something. For example, you might pay your child an allowance of $5 per week. A job well done for the week might warrant a bonus of a dollar or two. Use an amount that fits into your budget and is commensurate with what your child would be satisfied with.

Your Child's Income Sources

At some point, you may wish to assist your young child in finding alternative income sources other than family. At this stage, their income is likely derived from the following:

• An allowance;
• Remuneration for household chores (in addition to their allowance); and/or
• Cash gifts from you, your spouse, step-parents, grand-parents, and others.

Consider opening your child's eyes to the plentiful opportunities and activities that will generate extra income for the products and services they desire. Always be sure that your child can handle these activities based on their maturity level and always think of safety first. These activities should be light during the ages of six to ten and this exercise should prove to be an experience in creativity as opposed to a forced "job." Temporary yet simple tasks for your child might include:

• Snow shovelling, leaf raking, or lawn cutting and trimming for neighbors;
• Setting up a DVD player or VCR for friends, family, and neighbors (kids tend to be little geniuses with electronics);
• Teaching neighbors or friends how to use the Internet, the basics of e-mailing, and other programs; and
• Something as simple as a lemonade stand as mentioned previously.

Helping your child find money from sources other than family will allow them to fully understand the power of exchange. It will also empower them to control their financial destiny, to some small degree, as you assist them in ways of increasing their education. As a parent, you may not wish to purchase all that your child wishes in a given year or maybe you don't have the budget to do so. Allowing your child to control their spending and design stimulating alternative income sources is a lesson that will flex their creative muscles and provide examples that will serve them into adulthood.

The Family Money Meeting

I didn't prescribe a family money meeting in section one because children under five years old are usually too young to understand and appreciate them. Furthermore, with limited income being generated and having only a piggy bank, the need isn't there.

I do suggest that at some point between the ages of six and ten that you consider a regular family money meeting. This meeting could take less than five minutes to discuss accumulation and spending between your child's accounts or it could be a longer monthly meeting to teach new money lessons. The point is to set up a regular meeting time where goals, questions, and feelings about money can be discussed. As your child enters their teen years—a time of more complexity regarding money—these meetings will become more important, but the habit needs to be formed now.

The rules for the meeting and how often you have them are up to you. Perhaps have one big family meeting and then spend a little one-on-one time with each child. Schedule when the money games will be played, update and re-read actions listed in your child's goal books, set your next meeting date, and log feelings and progress discussed in each meeting.

Lessons in Kindness

Consider making generosity an important lesson to teach your child each year of their life. Just like in the earlier story of the father and son sharing balloons with the seniors' residence, what small acts could you do while having your child witness the effects? There's no greater feeling than extending love and generosity to your fellow human beings with a selfless act that need not cost more than a few dollars if anything at all—perhaps just your consideration and a few moments of your time.

The most memorable acts of kindness bestowed upon me simply took a few moments of the person's day, but their love is still felt and remembered in my life. I recall one Christmas when I was rushing to get my banking done on Christmas Eve.

As you can imagine, so were dozens of others at that location. A very sweet older man just kept letting all of us "younger folks" sneak in front of him. When I asked why, he simply stated that he knew we had to get back to our work and families and he was retired with "all the time in the world."

Another extremely fond moment of mine was when I was having a particularly bad morning. I was in a daze ordering my coffee from a drive-up window, when it was my time to pay, the cashier politely informed me that my order was "no charge." When I inquired further, she told me that the man in front of me had paid for my coffee. I've never been so quickly lifted out of a pre-work daze. As I saw the van in front of me drive away, I noticed that it was rusted so badly and was in such poor condition, one might wonder how it was working at all. I, on the other hand, was driving a brand-new luxury car. Why would this man, whom I didn't know and would never be able to thank, bestow kindness on someone he didn't even know but who needed a loving gesture that morning?

When was the last time you were grocery shopping on a cold winter's day only to realize that you didn't have a quarter for the shopping cart? Has anyone ever just given you theirs without asking for the dollar back?

Although your child likely enjoys receiving things, if you actively conduct random acts of kindness with them, I'm sure they'll be hooked on the feeling of giving back as well. If the act of kindness involves money, remind your child how much delight they feel finding money and that sharing the feeling with others in an anonymous way is the essence of abundance. Here is a list of suggestions:

Leave your quarter. The next time you're shopping at a
    grocery store that requires you to deposit a quarter to

use the cart, leave the coin inside. It's not much, but the surprised shopper who finds the shopping cart for free will be thrilled. I've witnessed this sitting in my car and I'm always amazed at how delighted people can be at finding this very small financial treasure.

Give money freely. The next time someone on the street asks you for money, give them what you have in change freely and without reservation or judgment. Affirm with your child that there is an abundance of money on our planet and that there is always enough to give something. A caveat on financial giving is to only give when you desire to. If it's an act of love and compassion, do so with joy. If you feel resentment or thoughts of scarcity, don't give your money and instead give a quiet blessing. One can't force feelings of abundance and your child will pick-up on that.

Send money in the mail. Locate a copy of the white pages. Flip through the book with your child and randomly select an individual. Decide on a dollar amount for this exercise, which is likely to be $5 to $20 because we don't have bills worth less than $5. Write a note explaining your intention and that this is simply a gift from someone whom they don't know but who would like to offer some prosperity. Let the recipient know that you have not kept or stored their information and wish them success, love, and blessings—from one stranger to another. Can you imagine receiving $10 or $20 in the mail with such a note? No expectation, just a gift from a fellow human being. With most of our mail being that of advertisements and bills, what a treat and surprise for the person on the receiving end.

Send cards in the mail. When was the last time you received anything other than a bill in the mail? Receiv-

ing a card is sure to bring a smile to the face of the recipient. Make it a regular occasion with your child
after each gift they've received or dinner or party
they've attended. This is such a lovely old tradition
that's long forgotten by many. It's inexpensive and
easy to do.

Send an e-card. Unlike traditional cards, an e-card is free
and nearly effortless. For no reason at all, have your
child send an e-card to someone different at least once
a month. Make it a "first of the month" tradition.

Say hello to a stranger. For me, this is more difficult than
it sounds. My mom has a unique and welcoming ability to say hello to any stranger, any time. If you're already good at this, keep practicing, your child is
always watching and absorbing. If you're like me, it's
a small risk to simply extend a smile and a genuine
hello.

Give gifts. Drop by a seniors' home at Christmas and take
in all of the teddy bears and games that your child no
longer plays with. Ensure to have them choose their
toys with you, and again, have them give only what
they would like to freely. They may not be able to part
with everything you feel they no longer play with, but
I'm sure they will wish to participate. Take your extra
canning or even the holiday and birthday gifts that
you know you'll never use to a women's shelter or
youth shelter. What about cleaning out your closets
of fashions gone-by and donating them to Goodwill
or other wonderful charities?

It might go without saying, but I must forewarn you that
regardless what you give, whether time, money, or otherwise,
there are those who will not be overjoyed with your act of

kindness. I think the main lesson for your child is twofold. First, extensions of kindness are a reflection of the giver, which is not dependant on the reaction of the recipient. Second, if the principle of prosperity that I outlined earlier is correct, and what we focus on expands, how can we not receive more when we feel so abundant (even if we aren't) that we're willing to give what we can?

A friend recently shared a story with me about her ill brother. Her brother and his wife were quite wealthy, but he was in his seventies and his health was failing him. As a loving yet impromptu gesture, my friend baked a couple of casseroles and a dessert and had them delivered to her brother's house. Knowing how difficult it must be to care for an ill spouse, my friend also wanted to extend a little love to his wife so she wouldn't have to worry about dinner for a few nights.

A few hours after the delivery arrived, my friend received a call from her sister-in-law. A cursory thank you was extended and some idol chit-chat exchanged. The call was somewhat cold on the end of her sister-in-law, and just before hanging up, she snuck in a comment that hurt my friend dearly. She said, "You know, I thank you for the food, but it's not like we're a charity case and need the food, you know." As you can imagine, my friend was perplexed. How could this act of kindness be interpreted as a charity case? Everyone in town knew that this husband and wife were wealthy and didn't need food.

I have also informally interviewed a few male friends as to their stance on chivalry. When asked if they open doors for strange women (or even other men, for that matter) or if they take time to always open a car door for their wife or girlfriend, most conceded that they no longer do. When I had inquired further, they all shared the same response: they either weren't thanked or the gesture was totally unappreciated.

When I first met my boyfriend, Wyatt, his charm was refreshing and I was amazed that six months into our relationship, he was still opening the door for me wherever we went. I had also noticed during that time, that he went out of his way to open doors for many strangers. As a quiet witness, I realized sadly that my disheartened male friends were right. So few individuals returned Wyatt's gesture with a simple thank you or smile. When I inquired as to why he still bothers when so few acknowledge his kindness, he replied simply and succinctly, "It's a reflection on me and the type of person I am. Their reaction is irrelevant. I would do it if no one ever thanked me."

I'm not sure I would continue to practice an act of helpfulness thousands of times over the years without being thanked, but that's the lesson for us all when we see a display of love for others. Whether it's letting another driver in during rush-hour traffic or donating money or clothes to a shelter that can never thank you, certainly our blue planet would be a better place for our children.

Above all, the time that you and your child give is the best gift, and it costs so little. Many seniors' homes house residents that don't have any family or haven't seen loved ones for years. The gift of a teddy bear and the generosity of a small child can produce love and attention for these very special yet often forgotten members of society.

Your Child's Prosperity Action Steps

- Have you set up the targeted savings account and outlined clear goals and timelines? Did you determine a percentage split for the income into this account and the piggy bank?
- What motivational style best suits your child? Have you

tried both to determine which works best and when?

- Have you discussed a chore schedule for around the house? What amount of money are you willing to pay for an allowance or remuneration for household duties?
- Have you determined and scheduled a family money meeting? How often will you hold them? Will you have them at home or offsite (perhaps at Grandma's or during a monthly lunch together)?
- Have you taken a few moments to introduce your child to various acts of kindness? Can you think of more together?

Section III
Ages Eleven to Fifteen

Chapter Three
Building a Money Mindset

The Banking Game—Ages Eleven to Fifteen

I strongly recommend that this age group keep their piggy bank and targeted savings account as we build upon those banks with a third account: the long-term savings account. Although your child should keep a separate pot of money in their piggy bank simply for their own control and enjoyment, at this stage in their life, I would suggest a name change if they feel they have outgrown a "piggy bank."

As any adult ages, many financial experts and authors espouse living with less luxuries and allocating those few dollars a day that would otherwise be spent on lattes or other such extravagances (which I consider necessities) and use that money for funding retirement, paying off debts, or some other use far in the future. But teens and adults find that they need a fund for financial freedom and pure pleasure. Sure it's necessary to save for the future, but remember Bob in the introduction? One must have a little fun and enjoyment along the way without turning into Tim.

The Pleasure Account

Depending on the level of maturity and experience your child has with the accounts set forth in section one and two, you may wish to introduce the pleasure account around the age of thirteen to fifteen to replace the piggy bank in name only. I recommend at the very least that you consider playing this game along with them. It's in their best interest to witness you having fun with money and bringing more pleasure to your life via simple indulgences, and you might be surprised to find yourself playing for years for your own benefit.

The idea of the pleasure account and the piggy bank are essentially the same. The main difference is the name change, which is important because your child may wish to mature their accounts as they do. However, it's best if a piggy bank of some kind is still used. Find one for your purposes as well. You might search for one together at garage sales or you'll find a number of inexpensive ones at your local dollar store. Be sure to deposit at least $1 a day in your bank and determine how much your child will deposit daily or weekly into theirs.

The second major change to this "bank" is what your child will now buy for their pleasure—and without your permission. Candies, dolls, and toys are likely less interesting to your child at this stage, if at all. Perhaps movies, spa days, and other indulgences are goals for you and your child to consider and perhaps indulge in together. Ensure that both of you empty your banks at predetermined intervals such as every month or every other month. Create a list of desires that you would each like to spend your money on and enjoy together when possible.

Introducing the Long-Term Savings Account

The next account to teach your child is called the long-term savings account. In adult terms, it could be likened to a retirement account where the funds will not be enjoyed for some time but are saved for future sustainability or future rewards.

The long-term account in a child's world and for their comprehension would be to fund a financial goal realized in the next twelve months to several years. Such a goal generally requires more advanced savings along with time to do so. An example might be a school trip to Europe that could require hundreds if not thousands of dollars to fund. The same terms and conditions apply to the long-term savings account as to those of the targeted savings account, but a separate bank account is required in this case, along with goals and discussions surrounding the desired future expenditure. The only difference with this account is time. To a child, a trip to Europe two or three years from now might seem like a decade. As you know that the money won't magically appear to fund this trip, enlisting your child's co-responsibility and creativity for finding the funds will be essential.

This account will teach positive saving habits for financial goals that seem a lifetime away. Positive reinforcement and reminding your child of the benefits of their goal is essential. You might have them find pictures on the Internet or in magazines depicting their desires. Consider helping them create a goal board in their room reminding them of why they're saving this money. You could help them paste several pictures of their destination, the things they'll buy, and places where they'll eat while on their journey. Then the dollar amount and a goal thermometer could be created to chart the progress of the money collected.

As with Jennifer's goal in the previous chapter, please see the example of Emerson's long-term goal of saving for an upcoming class trip to Europe. His parents have agreed to match his savings dollar for dollar because his goal is a lofty one. He has identified that he will need $2,500 to pay for his trip and to provide a modest amount of spending money.

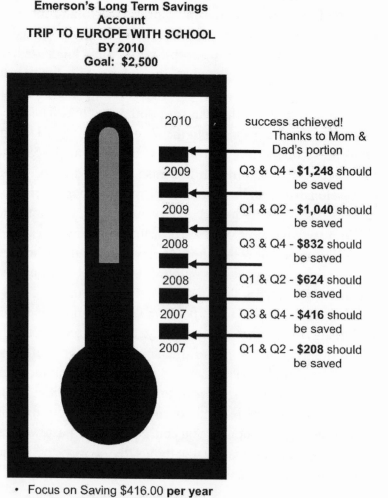

Emerson's Long Term Savings Account
TRIP TO EUROPE WITH SCHOOL
BY 2010
Goal: $2,500

2010 — success achieved! Thanks to Mom & Dad's portion

2009 — Q3 & Q4 - **$1,248** should be saved

2009 — Q1 & Q2 - **$1,040** should be saved

2008 — Q3 & Q4 - **$832** should be saved

2008 — Q1 & Q2 - **$624** should be saved

2007 — Q3 & Q4 - **$416** should be saved

2007 — Q1 & Q2 - **$208** should be saved

- Focus on Saving $416.00 **per year**
- Focus on Saving $35.00 **per month**
- Focus on Saving $1.16 **per day**
- Mom & Dad agreed to match savings to a maximum of $416.00 per year

With its high dollar amount and lengthy time frame, this goal makes the thermometer even more necessary for Emerson than it is for Jennifer. Since even adults can get sidetracked with the instant gratification some purchases provide, young adults also need regular reminders and positive reinforcement to keep them on track with their goals.

Use the following example to keep your child focused on their progress and remember to reward them along the way with verbal acknowledgments, decorating their thermometer with pictures and stickers to break down the time into manageable segments. Your child will feel the goal is more attainable if the dollar amounts are portioned into annual, monthly, and daily targets.

The following is a recap of Emerson's goal:
- He needs $2,500 for his trip.
- His parents will match his money at a ratio of 1:1, awarded once he reaches his target.
- He will need to save $1,250 net of his parents contribution.
- He will need to save $416 per year over a 3-year period.
- He will need to save $35 per month, which is $1.16 per day to reach his goal.

Remember to visit my website for a blank thermometer to use for continued focus after creating a compelling goal.

The percentage split between accounts is up to you and your child. As with the second account in section two, it depends on the goals that you have set out. I do recommend an allocation of no less than 20% for each account. If you and your child have decided to fund a project more heavily therefore depositing more each time into one account, that's perfectly fine.

At this stage, we still want children to have fun with some of their money; understand the importance of saving for an event, product, or service; and to plan for an event that's further in the future than they're used to. As the accounts increase, refining the income split will require some planning and goal setting on the part of you and your child. Consider the following example:

Sample Account Split

Income received this month:

Gift from Uncle Bronson	$50.00
Net profit from shovelling neighbors' sidewalks	$32.00
Allowance	$20.00
Bonus for helping clean out the garage to prepare for a garage sale	$14.00
Found on the sidewalk while shovelling snow	$1.75
Total income:	**$117.75**

Split between accounts:
$47.75 to the Piggy Bank
$20.00 to the Targeted Savings account
$50.00 to the Long-Term Savings account

In this sample split, instead of guessing percentages, I first considered that Emerson needs $35 per month for his trip to Europe. Let's also assume that we want to put a few more dollars towards his trip, as Uncle Bronson isn't always around to give away cash. Emerson would also like to join the gym this summer and needs to save $20 towards his club pass, which leaves $47.75 in his piggy bank to spend as he wishes. Again, have your child help calculate the percentages required and feel free to alter them monthly or as their goals change.

Finding More Money

There are few individuals that wouldn't like to find more money. Pay close attention to the word *find*. Money is everywhere. We just want to attract and keep more of it—as an adult and as a child.

As adults, we know that there are really only two principles to increasing our wealth. Spend less than we make or make more than we spend. With these two simple principles, I offer you the following lessons in prosperity. You can play each game on your own first and then with your child, or you can simply start together. Think of both of these games as treasure hunts. The expectation is that you will actually find the treasures you seek if you play strategically, even while thinking up new rules yourself.

Principle #1: Spend Less Than You Make—The Anti-Budget Game

Creating a household budget is a sensible activity that's inherent in almost any money management book or course. Personally, I don't think they work. When you're starting to figure out where the fat can be trimmed from your monthly spending, forcing a budget can just create frustration and failure. Just the word *budget* can send shivers up one's spine, conjuring up images of sacrifice and rigidity. Conversely, how would you feel about "money tracking"? It's a system I've used and taught to many that transforms the dreaded budget into an empowering hunt for extra money. Who needs more rigidity in their life? We want money and the freedom to spend it as we wish, not a spouse or financial planner forcing our purchases into a pre-determined monthly amount. I'm sure your child would agree.

As a former financial professional and an author of several books on finance, I'm frequently asked about this financial imprisonment. During my professional career, most of my clients fell into the category of ultra-wealthy. As you might guess, this select group doesn't need to budget—they have more money than they could ever spend. However, unless this group recently came upon a windfall, the majority of them did carefully analyze and were keenly aware of what they spent each month.

Another point of dismay with a typical budget is the idea of setting a guideline of what's to be spent without having monitored what is typically spent. For instance, I can tell you that you should spend no more than $550 a month on groceries, lunches at work, and dining out, but if you and your spouse are currently dishing out more than $900 monthly, a reduction of $350 is unrealistic. You can tell your child that they shouldn't spend more than $50 a month at the mall and on movies, but if the actual dollar amount being expended is $250, that bridge will be a hard one to cross.

The key to enjoying your money while curbing unnecessary waste is awareness. Start today and for at least the next thirty days, write down every dollar you spend. This is a fun exercise to do with your child; you can discuss the rules at your family meetings. Once they've seen you monitor your own household expenses, including what you spend on them, you can then play the same game with them, using their own monthly expenditures.

Purchase a small notebook that will fit in your purse or suit jacket (yes, write this purchase down in it). Log every dollar spent, including pre-authorized payments, bank service charges, tips for the pizza delivery guy, and every dollar that you spend in cash, debit, or credit. At the end of the month, tally up your expenditures.

Identify opportunities to cut expenses, such as ATM bank fees or late payment charges. These can add up significantly and don't do anything to improve your quality of life. Did you know that you're penalized for paying your utility bills after the exact due date? When your bill arrives in the mail, and if you bank online, you can pre-pay that bill on precisely the date that it's due while keeping the money in your account until it's necessary to part with it.

Spend a week or two studying your spending patterns. Your task then is to see if you can reduce any expenditure categories by 10%. The purpose is to then save this amount by being creative, such as taking your lunch to work instead of eating out or purchasing flats of water at a price club instead of individual bottles at the corner store. The benefit is that when you find areas to cut your spending, you don't have to use that money for retirement or other savings, although that would be a prudent option. After saving this money, you could choose to spend it anyway, except it would be on things that bring you pleasure and value as opposed to wasting it due to a lack of awareness of where the money was going.

I love spending as much as anybody and would never tell you to give up such essentials as your morning latte, after-work cocktails, or other small luxuries. Life is about savoring your hard-earned dollars and paying attention to the details. Instead of the saying, "A penny saved is a penny earned," I like to say, "An unnoticed or wasted penny is a penny that could be used for something better. Awareness, not scarcity, is the key."

What are all of the creative ideas you and your child could dream up to cut your spending by a few percentage points? Visit my website for a number of creative ideas and share yours with fellow readers. I'd love for you to e-mail me all that you come up with at info@theprosperity factor.com so that we can share them with readers around the world.

Although there is a time for creating a household budget, I just don't feel it starts with early financial learners. Once you've completed my "anti-budget" game personally and with your child, I would then encourage you to create a formal household budget armed with the awareness of what you're spending and how you'd like to allocate your money in the future. There is a plethora of books and information on the Internet detailing how to set-up a traditional budget and you'll find those resources on my website at www.the prosperityfactor.com.

Principle #2: Earn More Than You Spend—The Economy Game

My earliest memory of earning money was when I was around four. It's one of my happiest entrepreneurial moments. My mom had purchased a miniature ice-tea set for me. It had a fully functional, yet very small, ice-tea maker along with the tiniest of cups and saucers. She had bought me an order-taking pad I had requested from her and I was ready to open my restaurant—a dream of mine at an early age. I routinely invited a couple of friends over and asked them to bring their quarters with them because they would be dining at my restaurant. Mom would brew up a sweet batch of ice tea along with a few cookies or muffins. I took great delight in writing up the tab at the end of my friends' dining experiences. Making change was often necessary, and enlisting the help of my mom to teach us all how to do that provided a fun and unique learning lesson about currency.

I know my mom lost money with each of my restaurant

sessions as, to my recollection, I never shared any of my profits and knew she wouldn't have taken payment anyway.
Nonetheless, perhaps this early lesson of thinking of ways to
earn more money had set a course of action in adulthood that
made a mostly entrepreneurial career possible for me. Although there's no proof of this and it would be impossible to
point to my childhood restaurant as a source of success with
money, it was a great start.

What fun ideas could you and your child entertain that
would instill a positive relationship with earning money and
charging for services rendered? Designing a restaurant of
their own could be entertaining. What about their being a
mini-server at your next dinner party? They could help with
cleanup after handing out appetizers and refreshing the punch
bowl for the night.

We discussed a few ideas for increasing your child's income in section two. The economy game is an entertaining
profit-making exercise that will teach your child creativity
and the power of receiving money from others for products
sold or services rendered. At this stage in your child's life,
their social network is usually paramount. Consider teaching
this game to your child's friends or family of the same age
group and have them play together.

Many adults find it difficult to take money or cash in exchange for a favor extended to family or friends. I suggest
that if you've often found yourself in this position, reconsider
at times the issues that might arise from this simple gesture
of reciprocity or giving. Consider the following scenario.
Your friend asks you to help him paint his garage. You willingly spend your entire Saturday afternoon doing so, and with
a cheerful disposition. A month later, this same friend calls
and asks if he could borrow your spouse's car for a few days
as his is in the shop. You comply willingly. A month after

that, he asks for a ride to the airport. All of these favors are done willingly since he is a good friend of yours.

A few weeks later, however, you and your spouse are in a jam for a babysitter. You have an important award ceremony to attend and your usual babysitter is sick with the flu. You call your friend, knowing that he is home with no plans, and ask him if he would fill in. When you call, he makes up some vague excuse as to why he's not available. How do you feel in this instance? How do you feel about your friend? The situation and favors might be different in your own life, but can you relate to this account? If so, what has gone on in my example?

What happened here was that several transactions occurred between you and your friend. I would suggest that a "clearing of accounts" is important for the long-term success of any friendship, whether romantic or that of a family dynamic. Let's assume that after helping your friend paint his garage, he reciprocated in some way. Perhaps he invited you and your spouse for dinner later, purchased a bottle of wine as his thanks, bought you some item that you needed, or, if none of those were desired or convenient, simply gave you cash. Let's assume the same after he borrowed your car and you drove him to the airport. The payment need not be level with the actual cost of renting a car or a cab ride to the airport, but some exchange occurred and the "accounts" between you and him were "cleared." Then, when you call him to babysit, and even though you know he was free, he says no. Now with these circumstances, you likely wouldn't be as disappointed or even angry as he didn't "owe" you anything. He reciprocated along the way and your friendship was clear of favors.

When I've suggested this idea to hundreds of readers and lecture participants, some feel insulted by my suggestion (and you may be another). You might think that this is what a good friend, spouse, or family member does. You do things for each other without ever anticipating a return. And you would be right—some of the time. I do believe there are times to give without expectation and that is at the core of a friendship. But what happens when one is asked repeatedly for support, whether it is a listening ear during hardships or actual free labor, and these gestures are never returned? I am suggesting that we all keep accounts of the good that we do for others. Generally, we don't even realize we're doing it, and when we don't ask for reciprocity or are too altruistic to allow a friend to "pay us back" in whatever way is deemed fair, we could be hurting the long-term sustainability of the friendship. It's a sticky point between friends and you might outright disagree, but before you do, please give this notion some consideration for your relationships and those of your child's. There is a time to ask and receive an exchange from friends and also to create a comfort in using your close network to generate both an income and win/win situations.

The economy game is taught by Fredric Lehrman, a wonderful teacher of prosperity and abundance. Have your child find a few friends or family members with whom they can play this game. The purpose of this game is to teach your child about finding new sources of money through existing networks of family and friends and to also become comfortable with taking money from them in exchange for the product sold or service rendered.

The rules are simple. Each of you creates a list of at least ten items or more that you may have given away in the past or would normally never "charge" for. Your child will now happily (and you will too if you decide to play as well) give and receive money from friends and relatives. Keep the products or services simple and have items that range from fifty cents to a few dollars or whatever amount your child chooses. Remember to ensure that your child is charging a fair price.

By this I'm not assuming that your child will overcharge, rather that many are inclined to undercharge for their product or service. Make sure that your child will at least receive their cost back while factoring in a bit of a profit. This sounds simple and logical, but I can't tell you how many small entrepreneurs never really charge enough for the products or services they offer. They often don't have a clear idea of what their expenses and time really cost.

Have fun with the game and feel free to set up a sample market at your home, where your child's friends can bring in their products for sale and discuss the benefits of the various items or services. Make sure that your child exchanges with cash whenever possible and to do so with a smile while receiving the money. Have your child thank their "customers" with a verbal acknowledgment and have all of their friends do the same.

With the prevalence of e-mail, this game becomes even easier but more abstract to play. Payment can be made through the mail or a PayPal account, which will reinforce the element of surprise when your child receives the money somewhat unexpectedly. Although it is not recommended that one send cash through the mail, most would agree that a few dollars presents no great risk, given the benefit it will provide to the person your child is sending it to. Ensure that once you've received the money in the mail, your child contact the buyer cheerfully to acknowledge and sincerely thank that person for sending payment for the product or service. Your child will enjoy the spending and receiving process and will banish any old thoughts that it's not okay to receive money from friends. Here's a sample list of products and services for your child to consider:

- Babysitting;
- Homemade cards, candles, or gift baskets;
- Selling their parents make-up, perfume, or cologne samples;
- Writing Christmas cards, stuffing envelopes for businesses, or helping with wedding invitations;
- Providing a wake-up service if your child is an early riser;
- Sending inspirational quotations via e-mail;
- Providing research for projects (business or student);
- Baking or cooking services;
- Canning;
- Paintings or sculptures;
- Creating and selling an e-book or special research report.

The list could go on and on. Take time to create a list of dozens of products and services that you and your child could sell. Each time your child performs a service or gives a product to a friend or receives one in return, explain the game and ask if they'd be willing to exchange money as part of playing it. You and your child will always have "clear" accounts with friends and will enjoy the process of helping each other gain pleasure from the giving and receiving of money.

If your child has recently moved to a new city, doesn't have a large number of friends, or would simply prefer to try this exercise with strangers, consider a few alternatives. Perhaps you might check out the costs for a table at your local flea market or farmers' market. You might also know of someone who already has a table and would be willing to "rent" a portion of it to your child. If your child is too shy for this exercise but is interested in playing this game, have them try to find someone to sell their wares at a market or other venue. Online retailers such as eBay are great alternatives if your child is computer literate. A face-to-face transaction, however, is preferable to ensure an enriching experience.

Another excellent idea would be to get your child's class or entire school involved. Consider approaching the principal and explain the economy game. Perhaps a small tradeshow with informal tables as booths could be set-up in the gym during lunch or after school as a way of teaching the entire school this unique lesson in buying and selling. Selling their wares and explaining the game gives parents and children a chance to help increase cash for each child to contribute to a ski trip or to purchase books for their library. Every child at the school who gets involved in the mini-economy will have their own unique outcomes.

The Art of Negotiation

How good are your skills as a negotiator? When playing the economy game with your child, explain the concepts of negotiation and salesmanship. Was there a time when you bargained in Mexico or at your local flee market? Many relish the opportunity of getting a deal while others wince at the thought of negotiating. Many people raised in North America have not been taught how to negotiate and it's almost seen as taboo to "bicker" with a retailer. However, asking for what you want, such as discounts for large purchases or a special request at a restaurant, takes negotiation skills and builds strong self-esteem.

Should you and your child choose to play the economy game, I think you'll find that it gives your child the opportunity to negotiate back and forth with others playing the game. Also consider that the ability to ask for a discount or request a return on an item at a store that didn't measure up to your expectations is a skill that can be used to get more from life. Employees around the world are at this very minute hesitating to ask their boss for a raise, and men and women alike are either staying in unhealthy relationships or avoiding re-lationships altogether in fear of truly communicating what they deserve and desire.

Consider taking small steps in negotiation if you're not a natural already. When possible, have your child accompany you on simple journeys such as returning past-due produce or other goods to your local grocery store. When was the last time you were in the market for a new bed, sofa, or car? Make a game out of every act of buying to see if you can get a little more simply by asking. Are you late getting to the airport while your family rushes off on holidays? Asking to move to the head of the line could save your family from missing your flight. What about large chain stores? Many will negotiate with you when asked. At the least, if you missed last week's sale, you might find the store willing to extend the reduced price upon request. Did you know you could ask for an inter-est rate deduction when negotiating your mortgage with your banker or an increased rate when investing in a term deposit?

If you're like me and are challenged by the process of al-ways asking or looking for more (and find it at times embar-rassing), consider trying it occasionally when the opportunity arises. Not all of us are natural-born salespeople or negotia-tors. Teach your child the simple concept of asking, even when others wouldn't dare. With the opposite of asking being giv-ing, be sure to assist your child in providing more to others and creating win/win sales environments. Consider these ne-gotiating tasks and others to help build your child's skills:

- A better grade—if your child receives what they feel to be an unfair grade on a recent school report, consider approaching their teacher with your child to ask for a better grade;
- An increase in allowance—just be sure to outline the in-creased expectation of duties for the extra payout;

- Extending a curfew;
- Time with friends;
- Television/video game/Internet time;
- Choice of dining experience—if your children always want to dine at the local pizza restaurant and you'd like to try something different, have them negotiate a compromise with you;
- Asking a local business to sponsor their soccer team and purchase new jerseys with the company's logo on the back.

Can you think of a few more ideas for you child to try?
- _____
- _____
- _____

Remember that your child is watching and learning from your experiences negotiating, as well. Consider the following list to try as a parent:

- Obtaining a better rate on your term deposit or mortgage;
- Asking a store to hold over a sale item or to offer the sale price if you missed the deadline;
- Asking for a gift with purchase—if you just purchased a new camera, will they throw in a case, battery, extended warranty, or memory card?
- What about a discount for being a long-standing loyal customer? Perhaps your cell phone carrier or gym will reduce your monthly cost or add in other benefits;
- Asking for an upgrade on your hotel room or flight during the family trip.

Can you think of a few other situations where you wouldn't normally consider negotiating?

- _____
- _____
- _____

These money games may seem simple, but they have profound effects. Whether your child grows up to be a salaried employee or a bona fide salesperson, they will always have something to sell. Why not assist them with becoming comfortable with the process at an early age by conditioning their subconscious with positive experiences for greater prosperity and abundance that will serve them for life? If your child chooses the path of a salesperson or business owner, they will have to be comfortable with receiving money or raising prices. But even if they choose to be a salaried employee, being comfortable with their self-worth will give them the courage to ask for that raise you know they'll deserve in the future.

A Brief History of Money

The word *money* conjures many thoughts, beliefs, and images both positive and negative. Money seems scarce by its very nature. Even if we subscribe to a prosperity consciousness, we must admit to money's inadequacy, as there's not enough of it to fulfill everyone's wants and needs. When a resource is scarce, it's more sought after and valuable. I find it ironic, however, that in Greek, *money* is loosely translated to mean something we think has value (or something that someone convinced us has value), but in reality, it doesn't. A better understanding of the origins of money can help us make the decision of what we'd like it to mean for us today and in the future.

Money used to comprise such items as gold, silver, and

102 — Kelley Keehn

other precious metals; salt, pepper, and other spices; and even tobacco. In medieval Iraq, bread was used as an early form of currency. Today, money primarily takes the form of a bank note. A bank note is called a bill in the U.S. and Canada and is used as legal tender. Originally, money was backed by silver or gold, but carrying around large amounts of precious metals didn't make sense and could also be dangerous. As an alternative, bank notes came about.

A note is a promise to pay someone money. Notes were originally a promise to pay the bearer an amount of precious metals stored in a vault somewhere. This is no longer true today. Our currency is not fiat money and not backed by gold or silver. As bank notes became widely used, they became accepted as equivalent to precious metals. Bank notes are now simply called money.

Bad Money Drives Out Good Money

I'm sure you've heard the saying, "Throwing good money after bad," as if money could be good or bad. Money *just is*, no matter how much we try to personify it.

The phrase "bad money drives out good money" comes from an ancient time when coins were fashioned by shaving, where precious metals were removed from the coins, leaving them useful as an identifiable unit in the marketplace. It was first observed by Copernicus, and was later noted by Sir Thomas Gresham. Gresham's law states, "Where legal tender exists, bad money draws out good money."

A common explanation of Gresham's law is that people will always keep the coin that is in better condition (less clipped, less filed) and offer the less attractive one in the marketplace first even though it is of the same value. It would be only a matter of time before the "bad" coins were spent and the good ones retained.[1]

Have you ever received an unusually tattered bill of money, the type that looks like it went to the courtyard after school for a brawl and lost, the type that's barely hanging on with Scotch tape on both sides? I'm not sure about your experience, but that's the bill that I always try to get rid of first. Somehow, a ragged $20 bill, perhaps graffitied with writing of some type, seems to have less worth than a crisp fresh one from the bank teller or ATM.

Definitions for Life

Throughout the pages of the book, we have and will further explore the meanings of money and riches, but we will focus mostly on wealth, abundance, and prosperity, all of which encompass so much more than monetary gain. I think it's important to start with the basics and ensure that we and our children understand the literal meanings of these words, then you can redefine them to fit your own life. Below are a number of important words that I encourage you and your child to define. Should you not have a dictionary close at hand, two of the greatest resources on the Internet today are www.dictionary.com and www.wikipedia.org. Please use several sources for defining the following words and aim to understand what they mean in general and what they specifically mean to you and your child.

Money:

_____

_____

_____

_____

Currency:

_____

_____

_____

_____

Rich:

_____

_____

_____

_____

Wealth:

_____

_____

_____

_____

Prosperity:

_____

_____

_____

_____

Abundance:

_____

_____

_____

_____

Today's Currency

Here I will offer a brief lesson in the meanings, images, and symbols for which the American dollar and other bills are famous. Why are certain presidents featured? What's the meaning of the pyramid and third eye on the dollar bill? Some answers are concrete, while some people, including Hollywood, can only theorize.

What is more symbolic of capitalism and in a way, democracy than the great American dollar bill? As a resident of Canada, I have noticed that Canadians are keenly aware of the value of the American greenback and its many nicknames. Did you know that in Canada, our bills are all uniquely colorful and each tell a story of a past prime minister (Canadian leader)? They also include parts of our legislature as well, along with other history lessons on the back.

Learning more about foreign currencies can be a wonderful history lesson and peak into various cultures. You might be surprised to know that in Canada, some years ago now, our country did away with our $1 bill first, and then our $2 bills. We now have "loonies," representing one Canadian dollar, and "toonies," representing two Canadian dollars. Our lowest bill is valued at $5.

Recently, a friend of mine who's a grandparent to two children under five was teaching them an early math lesson with our coins, which can add up quickly. She showed her grandchildren that the coins added up to $10, and then gave one child a $10 bill and the other child two $5 bills. The result was that neither child believed that the coins could be equal to that of the bills. Even children under five some how value dollar bills more highly than coins. How does this affect the average Canadian? I can't say for certain, but I can speculate that it has made our affinity to the U.S. dollar all that much stronger. I would also say that the American dollar would never be devalued in a metaphorical sense by re-placing it with a coin, regardless of the cost savings to the U.S. Treasury.

Considering the importance of currency and the fact that the American greenback is used and widely received in so many countries, take time with your child to explore the rich history that your legal tender is waiting to reveal. The following are some tips from the United States Department of the Treasury:

- Who's on the cover of each bill and how are they chosen? The law prohibits portraits of living persons from appearing on government securities; therefore, the portraits on U.S. currency notes are of deceased persons whose places in history the American people know well.
- The basic face and back designs of all denominations of U.S. paper currency in circulation today were selected in 1928, although they were modified to improve security against counterfeiting starting in 1996. A committee appointed to study such matters made those choices. The only exception is the reverse design of the $1 bill. Unfortunately, however, records do not suggest why certain presidents and statesmen were chosen for specific denominations.
- United States currency notes now in production bear the following portraits: George Washington on the $1 bill, Thomas Jefferson on the $2 bill, Abraham Lincoln on the $5 bill, Alexander Hamilton on the $10 bill, Andrew Jackson on the $20 bill, Ulysses S. Grant on the $50 bill, and Benjamin Franklin on the $100 bill.
- There are also several denominations of currency notes

that are no longer produced. These include the $500 bill with the portrait of William McKinley, the $1,000 bill with a portrait of Grover Cleveland, the $5,000 bill with a portrait of James Madison, the $10,000 bill with a portrait of Salmon P. Chase, and the $100,000 currency note bearing a portrait of Woodrow Wilson.

• The eye and the pyramid shown on the reverse side of the $1 bill are in the Great Seal of the United States. The Great Seal was first used on the reverse of the $1 Federal Reserve note in 1935. The Department of State is the official keeper of the Seal. They believe that the most accurate explanation of a pyramid on the Great Seal is that it symbolizes strength and durability. The unfinished pyramid means that the United States will always grow, improve, and build. In addition, the "All-Seeing Eye" located above the pyramid suggests the importance of divine guidance in favor of the American cause. The inscription ANNUIT COEPTIS translates as "He (God) has favored our undertakings," and refers to the many instances of divine providence during the government's formation. In addition, the inscription NOVUS ORDO SECLORUM translates as "A new order of the ages," and signifies a new American era.

• The vignette on the reverse of the $5 bill depicts the Lincoln Memorial. You may be aware that engraved on that memorial are the names of the forty-eight states in 1922, which was the year the memorial was dedicated. There are engravings of twenty-six state names on front of the building, which appears on the note vignette. As a result, only twenty-six of the states appear on the note.

The upper frieze of the memorial bears the States of

Arkansas, Michigan, Florida, Texas, Iowa, Wisconsin, California, Minnesota, Oregon, Kansas, West Virginia, Nevada, Nebraska, Colorado, and North Dakota. The lower Frieze lists the States of Delaware, Pennsylvania, New Jersey, Georgia, Connecticut, Massachusetts, Maryland, Virginia, and New York. In addition, the engravings show the abbreviated names "Hampshire" (for New Hampshire) and "Carolina" (for South Carolina). No information is available as to why the prefixes for these states were not used.

Lessons in Money, Hollywood Style

No medium or industry can quite capture the attention of young teens more successfully than that of the film industry. Some time spent in front of the television can be more educational than you think.

Consider watching the following movie together. It's not really a movie about the history of money, but it does deal with some aspects of American currency; for example, it looks at the significance of the pyramid and third eye on the U.S. $1 bill.

National Treasure (2004)

This is a movie about an ancient treasure protected through the ages by the Knights Templar and the Masons, hidden for centuries in an ancient church below New York City. Nicolas Cage's character, Benjamin Franklin Gates, discovers that the map to this treasure is on the back of the Declaration of Independence, and to protect the treasure, he must steal the United States' most cherished document.

Be sure to watch the DVD extras with your child. I'm sure you'll both find it quite interesting. The history lessons and games are unique to any other DVD I've seen. Take time after the movie and research on the Internet what your child was most interested in. Feel free to flip back to section one, where I detailed a domestic and foreign currency game. Using the help of Hollywood to entice your child to research further into history and money could prove to be a valuable project for you both.

My prescription for this next lesson in prosperity is to spend an enjoyable and effortless couple of hours watching another good movie together. If you've seen it, it deserves an encore viewing. If you haven't, you're in for a treat.

Pay It Forward (2000)

In this film, thinking of an idea to change our world and put it into action is the challenge given to Trevor by his seventh grade teacher. His noble idea is to help others by "paying it forward." This concept expands like viral marketing does on the Internet. As each person is helped, they are then asked to help three others. At its root, the notion is really about creating more abundance and kindness in your life by giving it to others. Essentially, it's an exercise in teaching your subconscious that the world is an abundant place.

What a novel idea to pay an act of kindness forward as opposed to waiting for an opportunity to pay one back. This movie is the perfect example of the importance of kindness and donating money, time, and more. As discussed in section two, what activities can you and your child think up together to pay kindness forward to others? And what positive impact might this have on you both for years to come, not to mention those you help and whose lives you might possibly change forever?

What You See Is What You Get

There's a principle in prosperity that I examined in great

depth in my last book, *The Woman's Guide to Money*, that warrants a brief explanation here. The principle states that "what you focus on expands" or "what you think about expands." When discussing matters of money—saving, spending, gifting, and earning—it's an important concept. Just as with the power of words as discussed in section one, our thoughts and our children's focus also help them in achieving their goals, financial and otherwise.

What if I said to you, "Don't think of the color blue"? What did you just do? You thought of the color blue. You couldn't help it, even though I told you *not* to think of it. Why did your brain still think of something blue? Our minds can't decipher initially from a negative command. For example, if you tell your child not to fall when they head out the door on a winter's day, although well intentioned, you could be instructing them to do just that, or at least to focus upon the negative situation. For your child to understand "not falling," they first have to make a picture of falling and then tell themself not to do that. But they've already made a picture of it. Similarly, with *not* thinking of the color blue, you had to first make a picture of it and then figure out what not to do. If you wanted to quickly control your thoughts, you could say to yourself, "Think of red or yellow." Instead of telling your child not to fall, perhaps the sentence would be better phrased as, "Please be careful and watch your steps as you head out today." The underlying message of safety is still understood but is done as a positive reinforcement.

Think back to the last time you bought a car. Let's say it was a red Honda Civic. What happened soon after you made this purchase? You likely started noticing all of the red Honda Civics on the road and thought, "Where were they all before?" I have always bought vehicles that at first I thought were quite exclusive in my city in terms of color, make, or model. I then found within a matter of a week or so that there were dozens, if not hundreds, of my "unique" car on the road. How was that possible? How did you and I miss all of those vehicles before if they have always been right there in front of us?

The same happens with people we meet. Have you ever met someone at your child's school, a social engagement, or a work function and you continuously bump into them in the following weeks? Now they're at the grocery store and coffee shop and perhaps their kids use the soccer field right after yours. They've been there all along, but why haven't you seen them before?

The point of explaining this principle is that there are people, places, things, and opportunities that exist right before us, right now, but perhaps we can't see them. Your child has a bright and successful future—if only they would "see" it along the way. Our brains are miraculous and offer a computer-like sorting ability called the reticular activating system (RAS). Out of all of the thousands of bits of information that we could be focusing on at any given moment of our lives (which might drive us crazy if we weren't able to sort this information), RAS allows us to focus on just one bit of information at a time. Like a supercomputer operating at a laser-fast speed and without your conscious consent, it organizes and figures out what to focus on and all of the other information is therefore ignored or deleted. This process allows us not only to keep our sanity amidst the plethora of information we're exposed to, it's also the system that allows us to pinpoint the red Honda Civic and "not see" all of the other cars.

What we decide to focus on, what we choose to think about, and how we carefully examine the hours we have in a day can change our future. Imagine if you were armed with this information as a child. This concept is simple, but putting it into continual practice is much more challenging.

In *How to Get What You Really, Really Want,* author and motivational speaker Deepak Chopra states that we think, on average, over 60,000 thoughts a day. The potential problem is that he also reports that over 95% of those thoughts are the same ones we thought yesterday. If we want a better life for our children and ourselves, we must first examine the root of potential trouble. I believe this process starts with our thoughts, is extended through the words we choose to speak, and then through the actions we take or fail to commence.

The 30-Day Mental Cleanse

Most health books that you pick up will certainly outline a cleansing system for maximum health and vitality. Poor eating habits, lack of exercise, and environmental toxins take their toll, reducing our efficiency. Whether it's fasting, doing yoga, or taking supplements, most experts agree that clearing out toxins will assist the body in creating a state of health and balance.

Think of this next exercise as a gentle mental cleansing along the same lines as a physical cleansing. As we age, the compounding effect of inactivity and bad food choices requires a longer period of time to flush out our system. So too with a mental cleanse. Try this 30-day detox with your child. Surely, their young mind hasn't built up the inefficiencies that adults deal with, but it's important that their mind be free, even if for a short period of time, of negativity and self-limiting thoughts.

Have your child make their own bracelet, and perhaps do the same. This is another great way to bond with your child. This game is so simple yet within its basis are the seeds for a great blossoming of the mind. Each of you should wear your bracelets on the wrist opposite the one where you would wear a watch. The rules for this game are easy to put into practice.

Each time you or your child has a less than positive thought, give the bracelet a couple of firm tugs. As Chopra notes, we think thousands of thoughts a day and most of those thoughts are repeated from the day before. The first step in changing an old habit is to become aware of these negative thoughts about ourselves, our abilities, and the world around us. A couple of tugs on the bracelet are a great reminder when these thoughts occur.

If your child is resistant to this game, thinking that their bracelet might be uncool and would require explanation in school, feel free to try this exercise over the summer break. This is a favorite exercise of thousands of lecture participants and I hope you too will find enjoyment explaining this game to your friends and family.

Although not that similar in practice but with a similar outcome, I'm reminded of a habit of Canadian billionaire Jimmy Pattison. If your child needs a little swaying as to the "coolness" of the idea of being focused, I'm sure pointing to one of Canada's most urbane and focused businessmen will help.

I had the unique and great pleasure of interviewing Jimmy Pattison for a newspaper column I was writing to cover an award the University of Alberta was bestowing on him that evening. He shared in our interview and in his award speech a ritual he has involving his watch. He stated that although right-handed, when it's time to start a new project with which he must stay focused, he will move his watch from his left wrist to his right. His theory is that it reminds him that he hasn't been fully successful yet. Imagine that, a billionaire who still feels he isn't fully successful in some areas of his life. He further stated that he rarely gets to return his watch back to his left wrist.

The choice of whether to choose Pattison's watch strategy or to wear a bracelet as I prescribe is up to you. However, the latter will work better for this exercise. Once you and your child have tugged your bracelets a few times, you'll soon realize that it's not nearly enough to just interrupt your old thought patterns and to become aware of your current ones. You must now go a step further and replace your current behavior with more positive behavior. Do you know someone who quit smoking only to replace that habit with frequent snacking, thereby gaining weight and creating a new, possibly destructive pattern? What if that person had replaced smoking with exercising, deep breathing, or short meditative sessions? How might that have changed the reformed smoker's body and experience? It's not enough to interrupt your thoughts with a tug; you must be ready to fill yourself and your child up with something better and more positive.

The first law of thermodynamics tells us that we cannot create or destroy energy; it only changes form. So what will you and your child use to replace self-limiting or destructive thoughts? This law suggests that we must replace them with something; they cannot simply be removed. The simplest thing to do would be to keep your minds focused on the opposite. As a parent, let's assume that you're worried about paying your bills. You're feeling stressed and you keep looping a scenario of financial doom and gloom, which is understandable. However, whether you're full of anxiety or are calm and resourceful, your situation still exists independent of how you're feeling. What if you stopped for a moment and focused on the opposite of not having enough to pay the bills. Ask yourself how you could create more income. Do you think it's possible your brain might come up with some solutions for doing so? It's hard to do, but I know that being in a more resourceful state is better for your health and well-being, and will put you in a position to help you come up with a solution.

Suppose your child is fretting about a test coming up in the next week, and is vocalizing their impeding fear and likelihood of failure. Have them interrupt this thought with a tug and then focus on the opposite. Ask them about all of the things they could think about or do leading up to the test to increase their chances of success. If they answer, "Nothing, I'm hopeless," or something to the effect, just keep repeating the question. Sooner or later, their mind will formulate an answer. And with this positive directive questioning, they'll come up with a constructive solution. If they're still unable to state a positive response, give them a few options to consider. Could they forego the movies this weekend or have someone cover their shift at their after-school job so they can fully focus on studying? If you're willing, you could find a tutor or one of their friends proficient in the material who's willing to assist them.

Instead of your child beating themself up for a poor presentation in class, or you for blowing a sales call, you could both give your bracelets a tug and focus on all the ways you could have handled yourselves more confidently and what you'll do differently next time.

I write these words on my fifteenth mental cleanse in progress. Sometimes I do it for the full thirty days, longer, or just a week or so, depending on how much I need the reminder. The first time I tried this exercise, I needed many reminders. It also took some time to get used to wearing the bracelet and to remember to tug on it. I wore my bracelet for forty-two days on my first round. Whenever friends and family asked about it, it gave me the perfect opportunity to teach them the game I was now playing with my thoughts. I encourage you and your child, if they're brave enough, to do the same. By teaching this concept to others, it reinforces the lessons within one's own mind.

The second time I was ready for a mental cleanse (just as with a physical cleanse, once is never enough), I found myself tugging on the bracelet much less. By the third time I tried this game, I found that just looking at the bracelet was enough to remind me of my thoughts and my absolute power to change and control them at any time and within a moment. How freeing it is to remember that our thoughts are one of the few things in life that we absolutely control. We can't always control most of what happens in our lives; family, friends, work, and school often take on powers of their own, but our thoughts are always under our command.

The Importance of Gratitude

Sometimes, simply thinking the opposite just won't work for you and your child under certain circumstances. Perhaps your negative thoughts concern the loss of a loved one or a job. Maybe your child is overcome with worry about a potential bully or a friend who has shunned them. Or maybe these thoughts, on the part of either of you, are simply a session of self-pity, which happens to everyone at times. Gratitude is the great rescuer during feelings of disappointment.

During times of negative mental loops, where you just keep replaying criticisms or reliving moments that no longer serve you, look around at all that you have and focus on being grateful if you can't focus on being positive. This is often a new technique for adults to consciously be aware of and it's something that has an incredible impact. If pausing for gratitude is new for you, acquaint yourself with this empowering technique and then teach it to your child. I imagine that you wouldn't let your child keep watching a movie that they despise—one filled with negativity and despair—so why would you keep playing that movie over and over in your mind when you wouldn't desire the same effect for them?

If you read these pages on American or Canadian soil, there are likely millions (if not billions) of people who would gladly take your place for the chance to live on "free" land, a place of endless opportunity and resources. Imagine your life without running water, a heated home, or the political freedom to criticize your government without fear of severe repercussions. Assist your child in understanding how those before us lived and the sacrifices they made so that we could live in an environment where we can afford to be ungrateful. If you have the gift of sight, can hear, have fully functioning arms and legs, you are truly blessed indeed. It's often said that if everyone threw their problems into the middle of the floor, you would gladly take your own problems back. During these often-difficult teenage years, help your child realize all that they have as well. Help them focus on what they're grateful for in life and watch how both of you attract more of it.

Why is it that we're often the most appreciative and grateful for what we've lost? When a loved one is gone, we think of how precious those times with them were. When a leg or arm is broken, we truly appreciate everything our limbs enable us to do. When we appreciate life and all that we have, we focus on the now and receive all of the blessings of doing so.

The final method for replacing unconstructive thought patterns without the bracelet exercise involves living a day as your hero. Have your child do the same. We all have conversations with ourselves in the form of self-talk. When you converse with yourself, it's as though two different people are speaking to each other. Think of someone you greatly admire—either living or dead—with whom you wouldn't hesitate spending a day if you had the opportunity.

Now practice your self-talk, and when you do, converse only in your head as though you were speaking to your hero. If your hero were self-reproachful about a bad speech or, in the case of your child's hero, for flunking an exam, would you allow it? No, you'd console your hero by pointing out how great the talk went or focus on the positive aspects of the exam. You'd stress the positive and how there will be many opportunities in the future to do better or that in the long run, it doesn't really matter that much.

What if your hero was over for a dinner party and spilled red wine and lasagne on your newly cleaned cream-colored carpet? Remember, this is someone you adore and it thrills you being in their presence. Would you lose your temper or would you insist that it wasn't that big a deal? I'll guess the latter, but what if that was your spouse that did the same thing while eating in the living room or your child racing through with a friend? How controlled would your anger be at that point? What if it was you who spilled the wine and pasta? How might you react? If you agree that you would downplay the accident with your hero regarding their blunder, why wouldn't you extend the same love to your spouse, your child, or yourself? Treat and talk to yourself, and those important to you, as though they were your greatest heroes on earth. Encourage your child to do the same and set the stage for them as a role model for this incredibly important lesson.

Financial Goal Setting: The Seven Steps

Many adults find goal setting laborious and onerous. It needn't be that way. The following are some simple tips for setting financial goals with your child. The most important part of the process is to set a goal, write it down, and monitor it. It's important to understand how to get from point A (where your child is now) to point B (where they'd like to go). As essential as goal setting is for a greater probability of success, so is the necessity to make each goal attainable. Too often, a lofty ideal is plucked out of thin air with little likelihood of attainability. Such a process can be dangerous. If a goal is set too high, your child will feel a sense of failure before even trying. Set realistic goals with your child and raise the bar as each goal is achieved.

Your child has two things in common with every millionaire and billionaire in the world. The first thing being their own thoughts. Your child has absolute control over what they choose to think about but may need you to help direct their focus. The second thing is the 24 hours in a day. Not one life is created equal. Some have opportunities presented to them and others must rise above great inequalities. But, to be sure, two things will always remain equal and within the control of each and every human being: our thoughts and our time. How we choose to spend and nurture each of these will in great part determine our success, including the success of your child.

Step #1: Define Success and Each Goal Clearly

What does success mean to you and your child? Is it a dollar amount, education, a physical state, or a career status? Is it being a successful parent, a loving family member, or is it having many long-term relationships? I personally prefer author Earl Nightingale's definition of success. To paraphrase, he states in *Lead the Field* that a person is successful when they are focused on the attainment of a worthy goal. By this definition, as long as we have a goal and are working to actualize it, we are successful. Achieving a goal is to be celebrated indeed and deserves a pat on the back. However, new and more challenging goals need to be set for continued success. To add another definition of success, Lou Holtz, ex-coach of the famed Notre Dame football team, states, "Success is only for the moment." One should realize that a triumphant life encompasses so much more than wealth, sports victories, or other achievements. There's no right or wrong definition of success or a successful life, but to define this with your child and determine your own meaning is important.

Step #2: Why Haven't You Set Your Goals?

If your child hasn't set clear goals, why not? Most simply stated, fear is the common root of what halts most individuals from sitting down with a pen and paper to set out a path to a better life. Through these simple steps, you and your child will set your goals out in front of you, but it is a valuable exercise to also examine what it is that might be holding you back. Once you overcome your fears, setting goals will be easier than you had anticipated.

Step #3: It All Starts with the 24 Hours You Have

Don't let your child fall prey to the "*one* day I'll..." and "I *should* do..." We all have the same 24 hours in a day and we have more free time than ever in history, yet so many seem busier than ever. Calculate with your child how much time is spent in a given year sleeping and going to school and then calculate the total hours available to them in the same year. I think you'll both be shocked at how many free hours are available to them. Discuss how many hours per day, week, or month will then be allocated towards their goals.

Step #4: Set Realistic Goals

Setting high standards for your child is a worthy cause indeed, but you should be sure they are realistic. If goals are too lofty and unattainable, your child might not even participate. Remember, once each goal is achieved, new ones can be set.

Step #5: Celebrate Along the Way

Setting goals is important, but outlining how you will cel-

ebrate should be recorded next to the goal as well. With financial goals, this is relatively simple because the attained
result is usually the reward. For instance, if your child is saving for a school trip to Europe in the next two years and at the
end of the time period actually saves enough, the reward and
celebration would be the trip itself. But what about non-fi-
nancial goals? This 7-step process works for any desire, but
a celebration must accompany the successful completion. For
instance, if your child's goal is to increase their grade average from a B- to an A, what benefits and rewards will be waiting at the end of their successful journey? Ensure that these
are compelling to your child and review the "away from" and
"towards" motivational styles referred to in section two.

Step #6: The Acid Test

To gauge their likelihood for success, your child's goals
must be "tested" against other life goals and daily tasks. For
instance, your child may have a goal of saving up several
thousands of dollars for their first car when they turn sixteen.
Together you may have detailed the extra hours they'll have
to work to achieve that goal. You may discover that in order
for them to reach this goal at sixteen, they'll need to forfeit
their other desire to travel to Europe in addition to missing
soccer games and other events, possibly having their marks
slip, and being behind in their homework.

These are just assumptions, but by thinking forward as to
what will have to be given up by your child for the attainment of a car, they may not be willing to give up things they
didn't originally consider. Perhaps the goal deadline should
be postponed to the age of eighteen so they won't need to
give up as much during the years of saving, or maybe the
amount they'd like to spend on the car should be reduced.
Perhaps you both could think of a creative idea for working

less but smarter. Maybe your child could spend their summer job at a car dealership and work out a better deal on a car for less. The main point is to have your child work through any potential conflicts the goal may create.

Step #7: Take Action Now!

Once your child's goal setting process has been completed, there's a new process that you'll need to follow.

- *Measure progress.* This can be done together during your family meetings. Help keep your child's eye on their desires by measuring how close they are to their goal through all of the steps they've taken. If your child has moved off course, use positive reinforcement to get them back on track. Like any good pilot, they must navigate and reset their course to unforeseen circumstances such as weather conditions. Help your child adjust their path as necessary.
- *Specificity.* Is your child's goal specific enough? If they'd like to travel in the future, where will they go? How much will it cost? Who will go with them? When would they like to go? Creating a clear picture with all of the details will help your child focus more on the desired outcome. Qualify and quantify as much as possible.
- *Time frames.* I believe that the old saying "There are no unrealistic goals, only unrealistic time frames" is sage advice to impart to your child. Examine the time frames for each of your child's goals and discuss how realistic they are. If your child has only nebulous references to the achievement of their goals, help them attach specific dates to each.

- *Documentation.* Have your child write down their goals in a central goal book. For hard-to-reach long-term wants, have fun with their bank account passbook and write the goal on the front. Keep accounts of progress and use the documentation process as a small visual reward system for your child.

- *Get your child's hopes up!* I hear so many adults share a goal, wish, or desire with me and at the end of their last breath, they'll add in the qualifying statement, "But I won't get my hopes up." As adults, most of us have been disappointed and hurt before. We plan and strive for goals and sometimes we never reach them. We're scarred. The more we want in life or when life doesn't deliver what we had hoped for, scar tissue, in a metaphorical sense, starts to develop as a protective measure. But we shouldn't let this hold us back, and we should do everything to assist our children in getting their hopes up!

Think about the last time you tried to trick yourself in the following way. You were looking forward to something and then came back to the reality that you'll be disappointed if it doesn't work out, so you try not to think about it much. And then, when it doesn't happen, aren't you just as upset as though you did get your hopes up? It still hurts whether you were fully engaged or nonchalant about the result. I would suggest that if you did get your hopes up, you might have done that little bit more which could have made the difference to achieve what you had hoped. I certainly can't guarantee that positive and hopeful attitudes will help you or your child achieve their goals, but if your child is fully engaged and inspired by what they desire, wouldn't it make sense to try getting as worked up as possible if it would help them on their path?

Sample Goal Exercise #1:

Natasha's goal: Get better grades in school

Step #1: Define
• Move from a C average to an A average.

Step #2: Why Haven't You Set Your Goals?
• Simply start! Table goal setting in your family meeting.

Step #3: The 24 Hours You Do Have
• Today Natasha will spend an extra ten minutes reviewing her notes from class.

Step #4: Realistic Goals
• Should Natasha strive to increase her grade average to a B- and work her way up?

Step #5: Celebrate!
• Natasha just came home with a B+ on a recent report. Celebrate by hanging the cover of the report on the fridge with a bunch of gold stars and take her for an ice cream. Discuss her success and how even the slightest increase in effort helped her grade move up.

Step #6: Acid Testing
• Can Natasha move her grade to a B- in all subjects? Her math grades are consistently an A+ but her science and history grades are hovering around the low Cs. Will the increased focus on bringing up her science and history score potentially bring down her math score? Ensure to set a realistic balance.

Step #7: Taking Action
• *Measuring progress*—Create a goal thermometer for each subject and place them on Natasha's bedroom wall.
• *Specificity*—Natasha's goal is "to get better grades." We honed in on this further in the previous steps by specifying that she move from a C average to an A aver-

age. However, this needs further refining. A list of all Natasha's subjects should be examined. What are her marks in each subject and what are the specific goals to be reached in each course? A vague overall average of all subjects is not specific enough.

- *Time frames*—How long does Natasha have to improve her grades? Is the goal focused on the next month, semester, or year?
- *Documentation*—The thermometer or other visual aids serve as adequate documentation for reaching short-term goals. However, keep these and paste them in a large scrapbook or record them in a smaller book. That way, after a few years, they can be reviewed as past successes.
- *Getting hopes up*—Encourage Natasha as often as possible. Consider calling a meeting with her teacher and share the goals set forth.

Sample Goal Exercise #2:
Carl's goal: Get more active

Step #1: Define
- Join a tae kwon do school and shoot for the junior competition this summer.

Step #2: What Haven't You Set Your Goals?
- When Carl started at his new school, he was warned not to try too many new things at once, but it's now been six months and he's more settled in. It's now time for Carl to get more active, plus he'd like to meet more friends outside of his small school.

Step #3: The 24 Hours Carl Does Have
- Carl will search the Internet and see what information he

can find about the martial arts schools in his area. He can then find out the costs, schedules, and whether he can watch a class or two before deciding.

Step #4: Realistic Goals

• Carl hurt his knee in soccer last year and is very competitive in nature. Perhaps he should try out the martial art's school but not aggressively pursue the junior competition until next summer.

Step #5: Celebrate!

• Reward Carl for taking the initiative to research the tae kwon do schools. Spend a few minutes together after dinner discussing his new passion, how confident his training will make him, and the new friends he's likely to meet.

Step #6: Acid Testing

• Since Carl is competitive and sometimes overdoes it in sports, could the goal of training fervently for junior competitions have a negative impact on his young social life and health? Perhaps his aggressive goal will take too much time and focus away from his schoolwork. Examine all areas of his life to create a balanced outcome.

Step #7: Taking Action

• *Measuring progress*—Before embarking on a new goal, it would help to know where Carl is right now with his awareness of his physical activity (and lack thereof), the number of friends he has now, and his overall energy. As time progresses, checking in with him regularly and documenting his energy, weight, and number of new friends will serve as an effective measurement process.

• *Specificity*—Set an exact date when Carl will start his first tae kwon do class. Due to his recent inactivity, perhaps a class once a week is sufficient.

- *Time frames*—As Carl would like to enter the junior competitions, have him sit down with his martial arts teacher and determine realistic time frames for strengthening his knee and training for the competition.
- *Documentation*—As Carl feels stronger and his knee strengthens, he can increase his class schedule. Documenting his process will illustrate his successes, even if his days of inactivity are long forgotten.
- *Getting hopes up*—Discussing Carl's limitations and challenges with the tae kwon do instructors will greatly assist them in also encouraging him.

Your Child's Prosperity Action Steps

- Have you set up the long-term savings account with your child and outlined clear goals and timelines? Did you determine a percentage split for your child's income into this account, the targeted savings account, and their piggy bank? Did you decide with your child whether or not to change their piggy bank's name to the "pleasure account"?
- What money seeking-activities have you tried with your child? Were you successful in the anti-budget game? Did you try the same with your child's spending?
- What additional sources of income were you able to create with your child? Did you have them try the economy game? Were you able to enlist the support of their friends, family, and possibly their school?
- Have you taken the time with your child to watch *National Treasure* and to define what money, wealth, and prosperity mean to your family?
- Did you and your child find time to watch *Pay It For-*

ward? Have you tried any random acts of kindness together?

- Are you and your child still wearing your 30-Day Challenge bracelets? Has the tugging lessened? Are you and your child focusing on more of what you want as opposed to what you don't?

- Have you spent time with your child to identify their goals and run through the steps? A significant occasion such as New Year's or a birthday can provide the perfect opportunity for goal setting, but you don't need to wait. You and your child can make today the day to decide what you'd both like for the future.

Chapter Four
Financial Basics

For children and adults without an affinity for finances, this chapter can be a bit difficult to grasp at first. I've written this chapter exclusively for you, the parent, and hope that you will share this knowledge and teach the following material when you feel your child will be able to apply and understand it.

When possible, include your child in your financial meetings. If you deal with a financial advisor, accountant at tax time, or are in the market for a car loan or new mortgage, consider taking them along. Any new area of learning can be a bit overwhelming in the beginning stages, but once they've be exposed to even the bare minimum of information, they'll be more open to news/stock reports and other financial terms in the future.

I am, however, at the disadvantage of not know *you* personally. I can't assess your level of financial education and experiences so as to custom tailor the information to you. I've identified a number of major terms and financial concepts that I think are important for you to simply be aware of rather than be an expert in. I've attempted to explain these concepts simply and in my own terms. Please read and research further after completing this chapter if you like. There's an abundance of free financial information on the Internet.

The purpose of this section is not to define and analyze investments and the many facets of the financial markets. I intend to give you a concise overview so you'll be able to define them easily when your teenager asks about this subject. There are many wonderful books on the market that devote their entire text to the explanation of asset classes and our economy as a whole. If you're keen on learning more, visit www.theprosperityfactor.com for a list of recommended advanced reading and a chart showing how all of these financial instruments fit together. All of the financial descriptions are not intended to provide advice but instead a brief and simple overview. Always consult a professional before investing and shop around.

What Are CDs and TDs?

Two of the most basic investments beyond that of a savings or chequing account are CDs and TDs, which can be purchased at most banks and many other financial institutions.

A CD (certificate of deposit), also sometimes called a GIA (guaranteed investment account), represents a kind of loan to a bank. You are now the lender and are giving the bank your money for a term of usually one to five years. In return, the bank promises to give you the money back that you invested (also called your *principle*) in return for a set percentage for the term. Generally, the longer the term, the higher your interest rate will be. CDs can be redeemable or non-redeemable. The latter is most common and pays a higher rate of interest, but you're not able to get your money back until the term is up.

A TD (term deposit) works similarly to a CD in that your principle and interest rate is guaranteed for a set period of time. The main difference is that a TD usually has a term of one year or less. A CD has a term of one year or more.

CDs are suitable for investors who are not in the position to risk their original investment or those who need all or a portion of their money earning a set rate of return. The current disadvantage to CDs is that interest rates are relatively low and make these investments unattractive compared to others on the market.

CDs generally pay a percentage or two above current rates of inflation. During times of high inflation, such as the '80s, CDs were paying nearly 20%. The problem was that inflation was nearly 18% at the time. However, if an investor locks in for a long-term certificate when interest rates are high and they subsequently fall, the investor wins, as their after-inflation rate of return would be substantially higher. The reverse is also true. If an investor locks into a long-term certificate when rates are low and then interest rates started to rise, so would inflation. Therefore, the major risk with CDs is that inflation may increase to a level higher than the interest that you're being paid during the period you've locked into.

What Is a Bond?

Somewhat similar to a CD at a bank, a bond represents debt owed to the investor; it is for this reason that this asset class is often called a debt instrument. Think of it as a loan. You're the lender and the company owes you the money you've invested. Plus, the interest rate of the bond is commensurate with the issuer's creditworthiness. For example, a government bond with a very high rating will pay a lower interest rate (coupon rate) than a municipal bond. The lower the risk of the bond issuer, the lower the coupon rate.

Bond issuers are primarily governments and corporations. Bonds can also be issued in foreign currencies. A government bond will pay the least percentage rate of any other bond since they are the safest and their creditworthiness is the strongest (within our country). The idea is that a government can just print more money to repay their debt to bond holders. So if you own a government bond, you are the lender and the government is the borrower, and in exchange, you receive a coupon or yield for your money (the interest or investment return).

Unlike a CD at a bank, the primary difference with a bond is the liquidity flexibility. If you sign in for a 5-year CD, unless you elect certain options, you must hold that investment for the full five years. With a bond, you're able to sell it on a bond exchange at any time even if you had purchased a 20-year bond. You could, of course, hold the bond to maturity as well.

Bonds are very complex investment instruments and it's been estimated by many experts that the bond market represents over 70% of investments in North America; stocks make up 30%.

What Is a Stock?

A stock represents ownership in a publicly traded company. For example, ABC Bank would like to raise more money for current projects. In return, they offer a partial ownership in their company. Depending on the type of share class, the holder of the stock may have voter rights and could be entitled to a return of annual profits (called dividend payments). The level of risk for an individual stock might be rated from medium to extremely high. The chance for a stock's investment return (or loss) is based on the growth (or lack thereof) of the company. It is possible to lose some or all of your principle investment within a stock.

What Is a Recession?

A recession is a time of economic downturn, constriction, and the temporary decline of stock markets and the economy as a whole. It generally starts with climbing inflation. As the markets heat up, things start to cost more. Employees expect higher wages to keep up with the higher costs. Corporations' earnings must grow to satisfy investors who are always willing to sell their holdings.

When interest rates are low and the economy is strong, people as a whole feel confident about the future. Low interest rates allow them to purchase homes, cars, and other goods at reasonable rates. As inflation rises due to demand, the federal government steps in to increase rates so we don't see a repeat of double-digit interest rates like we did in the '80s. If you remember that time in North America, many homeowners were walking away from their real-estate holdings, handing the mortgage and obligation over to the bank or lender. Rates became so high and unmanageable that many people couldn't make their payments.

In today's environment, the federal government will try to stave off out-of-control inflation by raising rates slowly. In doing so, they intend to stabilize the economy before it gets out of hand. The hope is that if interest rates go up, consumers will spend less and demand fewer goods, and, as a result, the economy will then stabilize itself. It's sort of like pruning your trees. It's necessary to trim back the growth at times for a more robust tree in the future.

There are many factors and economic indicators that may turn down an economy, including war, catastrophes, unemployment, and much more. Basically, when a society feels poor due to low demand for products and services, the high cost to purchase cars and homes on credit, and a fear of low job security, this has a ripple effect on the country as a whole. The opposite is true when markets are swinging upwards and interest rates and inflation are low.

What Are Bulls and Bears?

Bulls and bears represent the direction of a stock market or how an expert feels about a particular stock.

A bull market is on the upswing. When financial professionals feel bullish about a stock or the economy, they believe a positive move forward is imminent and would suggest buying.

A bear market is moving downwards. Financial professions feel bearish about a stock when they believe it's ready to tank. In this case, they would suggest selling.

What Are the NASDAQ and Dow Jones?

We often hear on radio reports during our drive home from work or on the evening news the point gain or loss of these indices. I've included below a few simple definitions as many curious teenagers hear these same reports without understanding their relevance or what they mean. I should note that the word *indices* is simply a finance term to describe many indexes.

The Stock Exchanges

An exchange is really just that. It's a financial medium for investors to buy and sell their investments with intermediaries and some consumer protection in place, such as securities commissions and requirements for prospectuses to be filed.

Each exchange will have thousands of stocks represented and available for buying and selling. When an index is up or down by a certain number of percentage points, it's a fair but vague indication of how that country and sector of stocks is performing.

- NASDAQ—With approximately 3,200 companies, this index is the largest electronic screen-based equity securities market in the U.S.

• S&P 500—This index contains the stock of 500 leading U.S. corporations. After the Dow Jones Industrial Average, the S&P is the most widely watched index of large cap U.S. stocks.

What Is a Mutual Fund?

There are thousands of mutual funds to choose from and the entire concept can be confusing and misunderstood. Of the stocks, bonds, and other short-term, safe, and guaranteed investments that were not outlined previously, a mutual fund can comprise any and all of these assets.

Many individuals have preconceived notions, either good or bad, about what a mutual fund really is. Some feel that they can be risky, expensive, and better suited for *other investors*, but mutual funds can actually be safe or extremely risky, reasonably priced or very expensive, and are suitable for most investors.

Consider stocks and bonds for a moment. Each investment is as risky as the bond or stock itself. A mutual fund is a pooling of investors' resources. Some funds have only stocks within them and can be global, domestic, or a mix of the two. A balanced fund, for example, will have some cash in it, some bond component, and domestic and/or foreign stocks.

The benefits of mutual funds as opposed to purchasing the individual stocks, bonds, or other securities are many. Mutual funds provide professional money managers whose full-time job is to buy, sell, and monitor the fund's assets on a daily basis. Funds, unlike many stocks, can be bought or redeemed any business day. If you remember the Bre-X scandal of the '90s, there was a time when the company's stock was at an all-time high of $286.50. Due to the fraud findings, the stock was halted. That meant no buying or selling by the investors. Many holders of Bre-X stock watched their fortunes dissipate as the stock value plummeted and there wasn't a thing they could do. A mutual fund's units can be sold any business day.

Another benefit of mutual funds is the low initial investment. Many funds allow you to invest with as little as $500. Many investors would never be able to purchase a blue chip stock at such a low investment. Furthermore, funds provide diversification not possible with a small portfolio. One balanced mutual fund could have dozens of bonds, money market investments, and dozens or even hundreds of stocks within it. An investor would need to have a large portfolio to buy those securities individually.

Mutual funds can also be thought of as safer, in some ways, than purchasing stocks directly. With many stocks within a given fund, the likelihood of an investor losing 100% of their investment is slim. Mutual funds are not guaranteed (in either the principle invested or the rate of return), but with diversification, risk can be reduced. When you purchase a mutual fund, you actually own the stocks and bonds that the fund company is managing on your behalf. If they fold, it's only the management that is affected, not the underlying securities.

Purchasing investments individually

- Cash type e.g. t-bills and other money market instruments
- Domestic Stocks
- Foreign Stocks
- Specialty Stocks e.g. resource, green friendly
- Domestic Bonds
- Foreign Bonds
- Real estate
- Precious metals
- Index investments e.g. hips, tips

Mutual Funds

- Cash type e.g. t-bills and other money market instruments
- Domestic Stocks
- Foreign Stocks
- Specialty Stocks e.g. resource, green friendly
- Domestic Bonds
- Foreign Bonds
- Real estate
- Precious metals
- Index investments e.g. hips, tips

Mutual Funds can contain one, all or any combination of securities as listed within the circle.

Last year, a former client of mine was in a panic to purchase gold. She didn't just want a certificate showing that she owned a certain amount of gold, she was fervent about owning and housing the bullion directly. After counselling and suggesting that she purchase a precious-metals mutual fund that had a gold component within it, she totally disregarded my advice and opened a discount brokerage account. Due to the difficulty and logistics of housing gold bullion, this former client decided to start day trading gold, silver, platinum, and other metals. She started with a modest amount, and within a few months, had profited over $20,000. She told me that she "couldn't lose" and was almost considering day trading as a full-time job. She often informed me of her successes so as to point out that her returns would only have been modest in the mutual fund I had recommended.

After a few bad trading days and within a few more months, the former client had lost all of her profits. Over the course of a year, she was up and down as she roller-coastered between highs and lows. At the end of the year, she was now $25,000 in debt from her trading and had invested countless hours, causing her company to suffer in her absence.

The moral of the story is that individual trading is a risky game, especially with a short-term frame of mind. If this former client had purchased a precious-metals fund as recommended, the mutual fund managers, with their years of experience and education, could have mitigated her losses and even helped earn her a profit.

A disadvantage of mutual funds is that their management fees and commissions charged by financial advisors can be high. Times have changed, however, and fees are generally negotiable, so one must shop around. A further caveat is for large dollar amounts. An individually constructed portfolio can often be more advantageous than investing in mutual funds. Another criticism of mutual funds is that during a bullish market, one might be better off to invest in a stock index directly and save on fees. All arguments are valid, both for and against mutual funds, and should be carefully examined to determine the suitability for you and your child.

Why Are Interest Rates Important?

Interest rates tell us a great deal about what's happening in the economy and what could happen in the future. When rates are low, consumers feel more prosperous and will generally consider spending more if their job is secure (among other factors). If rates are low when it's time to purchase a home, you'll be able to get into a bigger home, have a smaller mortgage payment, or need a smaller down payment than if rates are high. Since a home is likely to be your largest lifetime purchase, knowing which direction interest rates will go is extremely important even though it is impossible to guarantee accuracy.

I've purchased two homes in my lifetime and have guessed wrong on interest rates both times. As a seasoned financial professional of over a decade and having researched and carefully examined the economic indicators that drive rates in the future, I still guessed wrong. A rule of thumb that sometimes works (but don't stake your house on it) is that the bank usually offer consumers what is in the bank's best interest, not yours. For example, if a bank feels that long-term interest rates are going to rise in the future, they don't want consumers to lock in now to a 5-year or longer mortgage. Think of it like this: if today's 5-year mortgage rate is 7% and the bank thinks that in two or three years the rate will be 10%, it's in their best interest to deter you from locking in as you would have enjoyed a few years at a rate lower than the market rate. Like any of us, banks don't have crystal balls either and aren't always correct, but they generally know more than the average consumer as to which direction rates are heading.

In today's lending environment, secured lines of credit (SLOC) and equity takeouts are all the rage. For a number of years, banks have been promoting the option of a SLOC as opposed to a conventional mortgage. This offers maximum flexibility because the borrower can pay off their SLOC any time without penalty, can use the "room" again just like a credit card, and receives a rate of interest at the prime rate or slightly below prime (the rate set by financial institutions based on the cost of short-term funds and on competitive pressures). The interest rate fluctuates with the prime rate; it increases or decreases along with it.

A conventional mortgage works similar to a CD but in reverse. The bank is the lender and you are the borrower. You choose the term (open to 5 to 7 years, and some banks now even have 10-year terms). The term is the amount of time that your interest rate is locked in, for better or worse, and the time period that you are locked in with that lender. The amortization of a mortgage is a bit trickier to understand. The amortization can be up to twenty-five years and, with some banks, thirty years. The longer the amortization schedule used, the lower your payments. If you pick a shorter amortization, your payments will be larger, but you'll also pay your principle off quicker and pay less interest in the long run. The amortization is simply a schedule used by the bank to determine your mortgage payment.

Let's use an example of a 25-year amortization on a 5-year fixed rate mortgage of 7%. You would be locked in to that bank with a mortgage term of five years. If rates declined in that 5-year term, you would lose out. If they increased during that time, you would benefit.

The 25-year amortization is only an estimate of what

your payment would be if you took twenty-five years to pay off your mortgage, if your rate remained constant over that time period. You are not locked in for twenty-five years; it's simply a schedule. When your term expires at your bank, you can renegotiate your mortgage or even move it to another financial institution. You can then recalculate your amortization and shorten or lengthen it depending on how quickly you'd like to pay the mortgage off.

What's Better, a Mortgage or a Secured Line of Credit?

There's no simple answer to this question. It depends on your situation and what direction rates are heading. Experts in favor of a secured line of credit point to the fact that in the long term of ten or more years, having a mortgage at a prime rate will generally benefit the consumer even with fluctuations. Furthermore, many banks now have some downside protection for consumers should interest rates start to rise and they don't have a fixed rate. Keep in mind that as prime increases or decreases, so does your monthly mortgage payment. That could mean a difference of a few hundred or few thousand dollars in a year.

If you're the type of person that needs the security of knowing that your mortgage payment is fixed for, say, five years and perhaps your budget couldn't handle a sudden increase of a couple hundred dollars in a month, don't choose a secured line of credit no matter what the perceived benefits. Consult your banker for the advantages and disadvantages of both lending options.

Compound Interest

The compounding of interest is a basic concept in the application of the time value of money. It is applied when investing and when dealing with paying back debt. Let's imagine, for the purpose of illustrating the massive effect of compound interest, that your child's school came up with the idea of collecting donations for a local charity. What if you told your child that the school collected an amount of funds each week that was double the previous week's collection? What if you also said that they were only able to collect ten cents the first week, meaning that the next week would add up to just twenty cents? Would your child think the project was a failure? Even after a few months of collecting at this rate? Let's examine the power of the compounding effect.

Week 1: Donations = $0.10
Week 2: Donations = $0.20
Week 3: Donations = $0.40
Week 4: Donations = $0.80
Week 5: Donations = $1.60
Week 6: Donations = $3.20
Week 7: Donations = $6.40

At week seven, this example is well on its way. You might notice that the compounding effect has only increased from ten cents to just over $6. Although a significant percentage increase, the dollar amount is still relatively small. Keep following each week and I think you'll be surprised as to how quickly the dollar amounts climb. Has your child guessed along the way what the dollar amount will be in the following few weeks as you move forward with this illustration?

Week 8: Donations = $12.80
Week 9: Donations = $25.60
Week 10: Donations = $51.20

We're halfway through our fictitious donation example now. I'm sure you'll agree that ten week's collection of $50 isn't overly significant, although it might be to your child. Keep reading.

Week 11: Donations = $102.40
Week 12: Donations = $204.80
Week 13: Donations = $409.60
Week 14: Donations = $819.20
Week 15: Donations = $1,638.40
Week 16: Donations = $3,276.80
Week 17: Donations = $6,553.60
Week 18: Donations = $13,107.20
Week 19: Donations = $26,214.40

With this example of how compounding can work with a doubling effect, we quickly move from a few cents in the beginning weeks to a few dollars in week six, to hundreds of dollars in week twelve and thousands of dollars in week seventeen. If the school were to collect at this rate for just a few weeks more, they'd be collecting over $100,000!

Unfortunately, investments rarely grow at a perfectly steady rate since interest rates and investment performance fluctuates. This compounding exercise is a simple illustration, but it doesn't factor in changing interest rates. What your child should extract from this example is how compounding interest upon interest upon principle adds up quickly. And of course, with the time value of money, the longer we invest or the longer our mortgage, the more that's earned or paid.

Using Lending Products

Bank Loans

Consumers seek bank loans for a variety of reasons. It might be for a car or to renovate a home. A loan has a term over which one must pay back the principal borrowed along with interest. Some loans may be paid off early, with or without penalty. The bank may or may not require collateral depending on one's security of employment, level of income, and creditworthiness. Collateral is some asset of value that a lender might require for security against your loan. In the case of a mortgage, the collateral is your house, but in the case of a loan, it could be your car, cash assets secured against your loan, or other such assets. Collateral assignments might be necessary for granting a loan and might even be required by the lender. In cases where the lender doesn't require security (e.g. an unsecured loan), the borrower may still choose to back their loan with collateral that will reduce the interest rate resulting from the bank being fully protected.

Credit Cards

A wide range of financial institutions in the U.S. and Canada issue credit cards. They offer the holder an amount of credit that can be used for purchases. The entire balance can be paid off each month without penalty or just a minimum amount each month (usually 3% of the outstanding balance). Credit cards have extremely wide variances for the interest rate charged for unpaid balances, which can range from 10% to nearly 29%. That doesn't include other charges such as annual fees or penalties for being over an established credit limit.

Credit cards are a useful tool to the disciplined holder. A major benefit to making purchases on a credit card is that it can act like a purchases monitor, keeping all expenses in one handy consolidated statement each month. Another valuable feature, which can be found on many gold or platinum cards, is a reward-point system that many companies offer that can be applied to anything from flights to various purchases. Other benefits included in some premium cards are travel protection, theft/loss protection, and much more. However, many consumers don't take the time to learn about these benefits and, if they are not used, the cost of the annual fee could easily outweigh their value. Always check the fine print and know the interest rate, fees, and entitlements of your card.

Mortgages

As discussed previously, a mortgage, in its simplest terms, is a more detailed and structured loan requiring a chattel against a home. Most banks will not lend funds or provide a mortgage for land.

A mortgage has a set interest rate for a given term (six months to seven years depending on the financial institution). Payments consist of principal repayment and interest. During the early years of a mortgage, the majority of the payments go towards interest. During the latter years, most of your dollars are paying off principal. Most mortgages allow you to increase your payment (so you can pay your mortgage off quicker) and also an annual or semi-annual lump sum payment (that is applied directly to the principal) without penalty and usually to a maximum of 10 to 20%.

Should you fall into an unexpected amount of money and have the available cash to fully pay off your mortgage before its term, you will pay a penalty to the bank called the interest differential. The bank will calculate this amount for you upon request. Should interest rates fall dramatically since the time you locked in to your mortgage rate, paying the penalty could be more advantageous than staying in at a higher rate.

Lenders and the mortgage terms they offer are more flexible today than ever. If you'd like to pay your mortgage off sooner, decrease the length of your amortization and make extra payments as set forth by your lender. These extra payments are penalty free and can add up to substantial savings since they are applied directly to the principal. Conversely, when individuals are stretched with their mortgage payment or would like to own a more expensive home sooner, they opt for the longest amortization period available to get the lowest payment possible. This latter group can still benefit throughout the term by paying down on principal during anniversaries or by increasing monthly payments where permitted.

Most financial institutions encourage consumers to make their payments bi-monthly as opposed to monthly to pay off the mortgage more quickly. (With a bi-monthly schedule, you'll actually make one extra payment per year.) Depending on when you receive your paycheque or direct deposit, you may wish to structure your payments to coincide with your cash flow.

Secured Lines of Credit (SLOC)

Like a mortgage, a SLOC is secured against your home via a chattel, but unlike a mortgage, it offers the consumer flexibility. Let's assume that you purchased a home for $350,000 by putting $100,000 down and choosing a SLOC for $250,000 to pay the rest. Think of this amount, or credit limit, as that of a credit card—just without the card. As you pay down the $250,000, you're free to run the amount up again, which, depending on your discipline, could be a good or bad thing. A SLOC also provides some contingency planning as you only need to pay the interest costs per month, which would be less than that of a mortgage (which forces you to pay principal as well).

For example, with an equal amount borrowed, a mortgage payment might be $1,200 per month (forcing you to pay interest and principal) where a SLOC may only require an interest-only payment of $700 per month. By paying only the interest on the SLOC, the balance would never be paid down. This is not an option with a regular mortgage. However, in a month of financial crisis, having an interest-only low-minimum-payment option as a temporary fail-safe could be an appreciated feature.

Remember that a SLOC's rate fluctuates with the prime lending rate, so if it's important for you to have a set monthly mortgage bill for five to seven years, opt for a conventional mortgage.

Equity Takeouts

An equity takeout simply means that your home has either risen in value or you have paid down your mortgage enough to build up excess equity in your home. Assuming a conventional mortgage, let's estimate that with your mortgage payments and house price increases, your mortgage is now only 62% of the appraised value. With an equity takeout, the financial institution will rewrite your mortgage or offer other options to use the 13% equity in your home.

Unsecured Lines of Credit (USLOC)

USLOC is similar to a credit card in that your limit and use is revolving (you can run it up to the maximum, pay it down or off, etc.). The difference is that you may or may not have an actual card attached to the USLOC. Maximum amounts are usually much greater than that of a credit card, but not exclusively.

An USLOC is not secured by a home or asset. The lender approves the USLOC on the borrower's creditworthiness, employment security, servicing ability, amongst other criteria.

As prefaced in this chapter, many assumptions were made as to your familiarity and experience with a broad group of financial terminology. In one chapter, it's nearly impossible to explain every money management technique. However, I chose those that I think are the basis of a solid foundation for you and your child. Please visit my website at www.theprosperityfactor.com for an extensive listing of books and Internet resources should you wish to study the subject further.

Section IV
Ages Sixteen to Eighteen

Chapter Five
Paying Bills and Using Credit

The Banking Game—Ages Sixteen to Eighteen

You will want to maintain all the accounts outlined in previous chapters with this age group, plus the addition of the credit system.

Unfortunately, many mature teenagers and young adults will consider the limit on their first credit card to be a target to hit as quickly as possible. It's not surprising considering the fact that personal debt levels in North America are at an all-time high despite our robust economy and level of economic prosperity.

Credit-card companies and banks are eager to offer their wares to your child at the earliest opportunity. As bad credit can happen to good people and a credit report can turn from great to poor with just a few missed payments, it's essential that your child learn the benefits and pitfalls of credit in a safe environment. I recommend a trial run for a number of months or even years before your child receives their first credit card or loan. Mistakes are forgivable in a test run but can haunt your child for years in the real world.

If you're wondering how bleak the debt situation is, according to a Newsweek article published on August 8, 2006, for the first time ever recorded, Americans owe more money than they make. Household debt levels have now surpassed household income by more than 8%, reaching 108.4% in 2005, according to a May 2006 study by the Center for American Progress. Consumer debt is now at a record $2.17 trillion, reports the Federal Reserve Board, and consumers cashed out a whopping $431 billion in home equity last year.[2] If we can hope that our children's generation will fare better in handling debt and credit, the lessons must start with you and at home.

Introducing Your Child's Credit System

This fun and flexible exercise will teach your child the benefits of using credit, how and when to repay it, along with the discipline necessary for using credit responsibly and the penalties that occur when repayment terms are broken.

Explain this new system to your child during your regular family money meetings. Determine with your child an acceptable mock credit card and available credit. This might be as small as $20 or, if you have the funds available, could be as high as $1,000 or whatever amount you're willing to "carry" for your child. You are the bank and credit-card company and you will be setting the terms and obligations for using and repaying this credit.

Discuss with your child why many consumers use credit cards, how they work, and the convenience they provide, not to mention the necessity of using credit cards in our society for booking hotel rooms, securing reservations, and much more. The idea behind this credit system is that there will be times when an opportunity is offered to your child and there's no time for you to save together for it or it's at such a good deal, you're willing to purchase it now for them. I would encourage you to instead use this credit system.

Let's say your child is an avid cyclist and their dream bike is on sale. The retail price is $2,500, but due to the new season's arrivals and a few small scratches that you're both willing to overlook, the bike can be had for $1,200. You both know this item isn't going to stick around at that price—it's too good to be true. You're willing to buy the bike for your child since they don't have enough in their targeted or long-term savings account to pay for it. Let's also assume that they've exhausted the funds from their piggy bank too. They don't have the funds but you're willing to extend the credit for this purchase. This is the idea of this system.

Although my example could have also been a purchase for much less, the same idea applies: there's an item you're willing to buy for your child which can be had at a great deal, but they don't have the resources to fund it. In comes the need for the credit card, similar to what we might reason needing credit for as an adult.

What Are Your Child's Credit Usage Rules?

1. Determine a credit limit. This is entirely up to you and what will comfortably fit into your budget. The amount doesn't matter as much as the rules and lessons for paying back that which was borrowed by your child. Also, set the rules for increasing limits (good repayment) and for decreasing limits or suspending the use of the credit all together.

2. Set interest rates for outstanding balances. This will hopefully be an enticement for paying the debt off as soon as possible. Take the time to explain that whatever item or service was a good deal months ago might not be such a good deal any longer if it takes too long to pay the credit amount off.

3. Set the minimum monthly payments. Determine a reasonable amount that must be paid to you along with how long the balance can remain unpaid (e.g. six months, one year, etc.).

4. Determine penalties for late payments or other abuses of credit. This could include suspending the credit account all together or taking on administrative fees for late payments. Try to keep the penalties as realistic and close to those of actual credit-card companies as possible. Remember to impose penalties only surrounding the usage of the credit system. If mistakes are being made continuously, review your child's income and re-explain the credit system and its purpose.

Let's look at an example of how the Bank of Mom & Dad's credit agreement might be structured:

- $500 maximum limit;
- Minimum payment is 5% per month of the outstanding balance (e.g. $25 per month will be required if the limit is fully used);
- Interest payments are calculated by adding 2% per month to the outstanding balance;
- Minimum payments are due at the first of the month, but bulk payments may be made any time;

- All privileges will be suspended if the minimum payment is past due by fifteen days or more;
- All privileges will be permanently ceased should the minimum payment not be paid for over forty-five days.

Have fun with the parameters and ensure they suit your budget and your child's situation. Here is a sample contract from the Bank of Mom & Dad. I would encourage you to make this exercise as official as possible. You'll find a blank contract agreement on my website at www.theprosperity factor.com or pull out your old credit-card contract for further examples and add any details you'd like. Keep this document with your child's other money goal books and review it periodically and renegotiate the terms when necessary.

The Bank of Mom & Dad Credit Company
Sample Agreement

This agreement hereby grants our child Harrison the following credit privileges:

- $500 maximum spending limit.
- Minimum repayment is 5% per month of the outstanding balance e.g. $25 per month will be required if the limit is fully used.
- Interest payments will be calculated simply by adding 2% per month of the outstanding balance.
- Minimum payments will be made by the 1st of each month to either Mom or Dad.
- All privileges will be suspended if the minimum payment is over 15 days past due.
- All privileges will be totally ceased and the need to renegotiate this contract will occur should the minimum payment not be received within 45 days or is continuously late. In any of these mentioned situations, the balance is still required to be paid off.

- If good credit habits continue for a 12-month period, this contract may be negotiated for an increased limit.
- The Bank of Mom & Dad hereby keep the right to revoke privileges at any time they feel this account is not being maintained in a young-adultlike fashion.

Signed this _____ (day) of _____ (month),

_____ (year) in _____ (city, state).

_____
Mom signs here   _____
                                     Dad signs here

_____
Harrison signs here

Income Split Between Accounts

With three accounts now and a possible line of credit (issued by you), a careful examination of the appropriate splits between accounts is needed. Ensure that all accounts are being funded at the percentage split to which you and your child have agreed. Set new goals or refine existing ones if necessary. If you find some accounts getting out of balance, perhaps your child's wants need to be prioritized if there are too many of them. Conversely, your child might have excess funds building in any or all three accounts, in addition to a clean line of credit with you. If this is the case, discuss with your child the importance of sensible spending or creating more compelling goals.

As we now have these accounts and a possible credit balance to repay, careful planning with your teenager as to their income and expenditures is important. Have your teen list out their income on their own and draft how they think they should split their money between accounts. Review their budgeting during your family money meetings, which you may want to hold monthly at this point or perhaps have mini-meetings as needs arise or income is paid to your child. Consider the following example:

Sample Account Split

Income received this month:
Babysitting (assuming $8/hour for 6 hours
      per weekend over 4 weeks) $192.00
Playing the economy game with
      friends at school:
        Sold 2 oil paintings $58.00
        Sold cookies and
           a cheesecake $34.00
Allowance (Mom and Dad stopped
      paying an allowance at age
      sixteen but still pay for odd
      jobs around the house) $0
Cutting and trimming the lawn twice
      this month $12.00
Money found while doing the laundry $2.00
Total income: **$298.00.**

Split between accounts:
$60.00 to the Piggy Bank (or Pleasure Account)
$87.00 to the Targeted Savings Account
$60.00 to the Long-Term Savings Account
$91.00 repayment of credit line to the
      Bank of Mom & Dad

In this sample split, instead of guessing percentages, first consider the needs of your child. Using Emerson as an example again, he's still on track saving for his trip to Europe. Some months he's ahead, depending on part-time jobs, and other months he's behind. Although he only needs to allocate $35 per month into his long-term savings account, when he drafted up the budget himself, he earmarked $60 this month because he wants to take July off to be with his friends. He allocated $87 to the targeted savings account because he'd like some new bells and whistles for his speed bike next month. Although he only owes the Bank of Mom & Dad $210 and his minimum payment is only $10.50, he's decided on his own to make a payment of $91 to accelerate paying this debt off. Finally, although he didn't explain this to his parents (and doesn't need to considering the pleasure account is for his own personal spending), he'd like to ask a girl out on a date at school and wants to treat her to dinner.

The Importance of Healthy Spending

Although many parents will find it hard to believe that there is such an issue as a spendthrift teenager, I'm here to report that there are such situations. Many parents dealing with teenage spending problems would gladly trade this situation in for a young supersaver. However, a lack of spending or a denial of pleasure can lead down a dangerous path. Do you remember the story of Bob at the beginning of the book? Although I'm sure your child's path is far from that of Bob's, small steps do make all the difference. Respect for money and a healthy balance of spending and saving are wise goals, but too much of one or the other can be hazardous to your child's future financial well-being. A balance must be sought between the two.

At this stage in your child's life, they may have developed slight or serious issues regarding spending money. If funds are tight at home, they might feel guilt or will want to hold on to the money in case of emergencies. Some teens may feel that they don't deserve to receive pleasure or obtain their goals, as other people are more needy. If your teen is having a difficult time using their funds on themselves, discuss their concerns with them and help them understand that money and spending can be win/win situations.

An illustration that might help your spendthrift or even your overspender understand how things work better is this simple observation that is sometimes even overlooked by many adults:

Money Makes the World Go Round

In the previous chapter, we discussed what fuels a recession. Although many factors are involved, at its basic root is consumer anxiety when we fear for the future and stop spending. If we feel poor or think we'll be poorer in the future, we change the way we shop. When we stop spending as a country, the companies we all work for suffer. Governments collect less tax and have less money for roads, schools, and hospitals. And so the cycle goes until it becomes interrupted.

When we spend money, enlightened and aware, and even if the funds are spent for our own enjoyment and pleasure, we're actually assisting in the prosperity of our city, state, country, and world. We're doing our part to help the citizens of this planet prosper, one dollar at a time. This might be a new mindset for you and likely for your teen. Think about it the next time you purchase anything and definitely explain the process the next time you assist your teen in spending any of the proceeds of their bank accounts.

For example, let's say your teen has saved up for new designer pair of jeans. You both decide to go shopping together and find the perfect pair at a boutique shop located in a trendy strip mall. After such a purchase, you should take a few moments to discuss the prosperity you have just had a hand in for so many. As a result of this transaction, the person that helped your teen pick out and pay for the jeans just received part of their paycheque. The storeowner is able to keep the shop open and the hydro and gas companies profit slightly too. The landlord of the strip mall will receive some rent and the government will be able to build another school this year in part from the taxes it received from all of the parties involved in that purchase that we only described in part. Let's not forget the Japanese workers and company owners who built and shipped all of the shelving in the store to neatly display all of the brands of jeans available. Certainly, we could go on and on. I hope that this example reveals to you and your teen the levels of prosperity extended to so many with each dollar we spend.

Paying the Bills

Paying the bills is a monthly occurrence that many consider drudgery and some others face with fear. This simple task might seem insignificant in your child's life, but the words you speak and the example you set can have a major impact on their bill payments for many years to come.

Let's define our bills in a new way so we can communicate this new thought process to our teens. I encourage you to sit down with your teen in the next month or make it an activity during your family money meeting to discuss bill paying and perhaps even show them some of your bills, how they work, and how they're paid.

What do you think when you receive your gas bill in January? Are you thrilled that the cost is ever increasing and likely double the amount it was in August? Likely not. What do you say and how's your mood as you head from your mailbox to the kitchen to open your mail? Is this daily session met with gratitude or complaint and frustration? As discussed previously, your words have power and your actions are liable to be palatable to your teenager. They're watching and listening at times when you might not be aware. I'm not suggesting for a moment that your bills should send you into a state of bliss. However, an awareness of what these slips of paper really mean is prudent and necessary to future deliberations with your teen.

In my opinion, a bill represents trust and a promise. A company has trusted you enough to entitle you to use their product or service in advance of paying for it. In exchange, they ask for your promise to pay for those goods or services at an agreed time. I think a bill is a lovely notion that credit has been extended in advance of us asking for it, especially in the cases of the hydro, gas, and phone companies. The head offices of these companies did not require deposits, credit checks, or any other requirements for their services; just our promise to pay in exchange for their trust. If that trust is broken and the promise not fulfilled, there will be repercussions such as lost power or suspended heat services. But the agreement at the onset is an honorable one. In a society that generally requires something in advance of offering anything, the fact that any company still operates on trust seems like a novel idea in today's corporate environment.

If that explanation isn't compelling enough for you to quit complaining about your bills (assuming you do complain) or at least compel you to choose more positive words during the opening of your mail, let's think back to my example of purchasing jeans with your teen. What if you thought of each slip of paper requesting your payment as a call to action, a request perhaps, that you help our economy by providing food and clothing to the children of your city or country? Even if in a very small way, the payment of this slip, this request for your money, has likely helped at least one child study with a full tummy or receive a scholarship for university. Would that reframe how you currently perceive these bills?

What If You Can't Pay Your Bills Fully?

Are you bad? Is that wrong? Have you broken a promise? No. It's not bad, wrong, nor has a promise overtly been broken. Then how do you explain this situation to your teenager? For starters, consider that the company and the people that work for them are still benefiting from your missed or delayed payment. If you cannot pay your bill at the end of the month, you are usually charged in the form of interest or some other type of administrative fee or set charge. To complain about these fees is to complain about the flexibility and options that are presented to you or the bill payer.

Ponder the idea that if these options for late payments did not exist, the gas company would simply flip the switch and shut off the gas. If you've ever found yourself short at the end of the month, especially during a cold winter, penalties for late payments are a small price to pay for continued enjoyment of the service. Explaining how companies work and distancing feelings of contempt for the rising costs of these services is an important lesson for your teen and possibly you as well.

If you're willing to show your bills to your teen and explain my previous illustrations, it will give them a sense of what might now seem to be a mysterious and vague "bill." Furthermore, it will help provide them with a sense of what it really costs to run a household. So many new homeowners are clueless as to the costs associated with running a home. This open sharing will give your child a solid understanding of maintaining monthly costs before they have to take on these costs on their own.

When Bad Credit Happens to Good People

People don't intend on ruining their credit and I'm sure that the vast majority intend on paying for a product or service after having obtained credit for them. Unfortunately, as the saying goes, "Life happens while we're busy doing other things." A life disruption such as a divorce, death, or job loss can inadvertently cause a few missed monthly payments that can quickly turn perfect credit into a sad state of financial affairs.

The biggest problem with financial troubles and poor credit is that it renders the individual weak in a financial sense. Just when they need money and the help of lenders the most, no one is there to assist. Furthermore, one's self-esteem can be battered during this time, in addition to having feelings of isolation and, in severe cases, depression and hopelessness. This is precisely when the financially downtrodden can fall prey to false credit reports, abuse by creditors, and the bombardment of bankruptcy commercials on late-night television, each of these telling them this is the way things work.

The solution always starts with awareness and education. Only when one in financial trouble knows their rights and all of the available options can their financial life improve. No matter how glowing or disparaged your own credit situation is or has been, it's essential that your teen understand that a few simple mistakes in their adulthood can haunt them for years to come. A simple lesson can ensure that their credit experiences are positive or, if less than perfect, you'll at least empower them with solutions and recourse.

What Is a Credit Report?

A credit report is a history of how consistently you pay your financial obligations. It is created when you first borrow money or apply for credit. On a regular basis, the companies that lend money or issue credit cards to you (banks, finance companies, credit unions, retailers, etc.) send the credit-reporting agencies specific and factual information about their financial relationship with you—when you opened up your account, if you make your payments on time, if you miss a payment, or if you have gone over your credit limit, etc.

Credit agencies such as Equifax receives this information directly from the financial and retail institutions and retains it to help other lenders make decisions about granting you credit. Since your credit report contains all the information received from your lenders and provides a picture of your financial health, other lenders will request your report when they are determining whether to grant you a loan. Your credit report is a history that will help them determine what kind of lending risk you are—if you are likely to repay your obligation on time or not.

Your credit report is like a financial report card. It outlines the status of your payments to creditors, reveals if and how often late payments occurred, and provides a basis for your future creditworthiness to lenders. You may obtain a free report by writing to these companies or, in our ever-evolving word of technology, can pay a number of fees online for a basic or advanced report. With escalading identity theft and the fact that creditors can incorrectly report your payment history, most professionals recommend checking your credit report every six months.

Gone are the days of R1–R9 ratings that the old credit-reporting systems used to generate. They now use complex scores that factor in everything from how often you're late on a monthly payment, the number of times you seek credit, your history (if any) with collection agencies, and if you're fully extended on the revolving credit you hold. The higher the incidence of any of these factors, the higher your score.

There is also something called "soft hits" and "hard hits." When you agree to any type of loan or revolving credit, you'll often find in the small print that the credit company reserves the right to periodically review your credit report. This would be considered a soft hit and would not directly affect your report. A hard hit does and could hinder your ability to be approved for credit in the short term or until it's removed from your record.

Let's assume that you're shopping around for a mortgage or car loan. When you meet with your banker or financial representative at the car dealership, it's essential that you ask them not to pull your report until you've decided to deal with them. With our current privacy laws, no financial institution or other body is authorized to access your credit report without your authority. However, in real life, this isn't always the case or, at the very least, some of these companies do not make it abundantly clear that they will access your report. Should you find yourself shopping around for such lending and innocently induce three or four lenders to view your credit report, this can dramatically pull down your standing in the short term. If other lenders think that you're seeking credit, they may raise the question as to why you didn't get approved by the inquiring lenders, when this wasn't actually the case.

What you'll find within your report:
- *Personal identification.* Your name, address, employment status, and more.
- *Consumer statement.* Where you can add comments about your report.
- *Credit information.* Details your credit amount, history of good or poor payments, and your credit limit and the balance at the time. (Your mortgage generally will

166 — Kelley Keehn

not show up on your credit report.)
- *Banking information.* Like the credit information, this section will track your banking history.
- *Public record information.* This section will list such occurrences as bankruptcies or judgments.
- *Third-party collections.* Should a delinquent account be sent to a collection agency for recovery of funds, this section would list the details.
- *Inquires.* This section would list all soft and hard hits to your report over the past three years.

Where Did Credit Come From?

In section two, we briefly examined the history of money. Knowing the history of the original credit card is also something of value to your teen and perhaps even you.

Although I never had a chance to meet any of my grandparents, I know that during their lifetime, and those of most individuals during the late 1800s and early 1900s, what you owned was what you could save up for or build over time. There wasn't an option of owning a larger home by taking on credit. It was a time of pure worth. Generally speaking, you had what you could afford. Certainly there were bankers available and loans and mortgages were granted; however, the credit landscape was quite different back then.

Fast forward to my parent's generation and the general mantra of that age group during the late '60s and early '70s: pay the mortgage off as soon as possible. This group may have seen or felt some of the lingering effects of the Great Depression that their parents lived though. Owning a home free and clear that no one could take away from them was generally the priority of this group of individuals.

I look at my generation and those who come just before and after and am concerned about how, within just a few decades, the use of credit seems dangerous in its overindulgence. In this new millennium, it seems equally important to know the history of both credit cards and money. As a member of the Generation X demographic, I sadly admit that paying with plastic (both debit and credit card) has superseded paying with real money. A history lesson is indeed in order!

The first credit card was actually created in the '20s and was used to sell fuel to a growing number of car owners. Frank X. McNamara came up with the concept of paying merchants using a card in 1950. The first charge card in existence was the Diners Club.

In 1958, Bank of America introduced their card, which evolved into the Visa system, and MasterCard followed suit in 1966. There are now a countless number of cards in the U.S. and Canada that are almost universally accepted in both countries. An economic agreement can be made whereby using credit cards increases the velocity of money in an economy, resulting in higher consumer spending, escalating debt, and higher GDP.[3] Credit-card debt has soared to new heights in the last decade and I'm sure we all know someone who has had to bear the tragedy of being unable to handle such debts.

Not everyone in the world lives as Americans and Canadians do. I think this is a really important discussion to have with your teenager, and if they're heading on a trip to Europe with you or their school, that's even better. As an adult, even I have a hard time with understanding that parts of Europe live so very differently than we do. I'm sure you've also heard the tales of short work days and weeks and enjoying long morning coffees, afternoon siestas, and regular evening dining experiences that focus on family and pleasure.

With several friends arriving to Canada from Europe both just a few years and a few decades ago, I wondered if these tales of a life of leisure still exist. When I inquired about this lifestyle, my friends, many of who are now totally immersed in our culture and working over sixty hours per week, took the time to relive their more balanced past. How can these cities and countries be so different from our rules of work and play?

After a little research, I learned that it's not as important for many Europeans to have as much "stuff" as we have. Consider that the average family in our country has a car (maybe two), owns a home, and has many bills to pay. The upper and middle class, even some in the lower-middle class, pretty much have all of the same things: a mortgage, cars, food and clothing, and all the "essentials" of life. The wealthy generally just have bigger debts, bigger homes, and perhaps just more, but at what cost?

Many citizens of balanced European countries typically don't drive, but if they do, they own only one car. They might never aspire to own a home, but if they do, it would likely be a modest structure. Family, a healthy social network, and time to experience life are more important than getting ahead in their careers or simply having more or bigger "stuff." Our desire to acquire more things, and to have it before we've even saved up for it, has cost North Americans dearly. So many dread Monday mornings and spend at least forty hours a week hating their lives.

It's important that our children understand that there is good debt and bad debt, times to use credit and times to forego the lure and temptation of having something now as opposed to saving up for it. When one overborrows for instant gratification or for more than they can afford, they enter a limiting bondship with the lender. In dire situations, out-of-control borrowing or unforeseen life occurrences can lead to bankruptcy.

To observe what is further perpetuating the idea in our

society that overspending and living beyond one's means is acceptable, one need only turn on the television in the evening or late night and be bombarded with commercials by bankruptcy trustees touting this process as a savior and a chance to erase all debts owning. There are times when life deals a bad hand and bankruptcy is the only option. Perhaps there's been a disability, death in the family, lost job, or economic downturn. However, a vast number of personal bankruptcies do not result from a catastrophe. There are many that result from overspending and overborrowing.

Bankruptcy is a serious process that one should not enter into lightly. The trust of a lender or service provider is broken when all payments cease. To be absolved of this responsibility can potentially have damaging consequences on one's self-esteem. I have counselled a number of clients who had no option but to file for bankruptcy. The blows to their self-esteem were long sustained, not to mention the negative impact bankruptcy will have on their ability to borrow in the future. What I was surprised to learn was that the clients I counselled who were least bruised emotionally by the process were the ones who were slowly paying back their creditors even though they didn't need to. For them, their word and repayment of what they had promised years before were important to them. Although their insolvency afforded them a second chance, they took responsibility for honoring their promises.

I don't aim to support the process of bankruptcy nor condemn those who fall prey to overeager credit providers or unfortunate life circumstances. The point is that children are highly susceptible to what they see on television. Countless commercials glossing over the issue of bankruptcy as though it were no big deal and that a "second" financial chance can be had easily could lead to irresponsibility on your child's part as they enter adulthood. Take time during your family financial meetings to discuss the emotional and credit impact that bankruptcy can have and that it should be a last-resort solution should troubles arise. Preventative measures, good habits, and respect regarding credit need to be reinforced with your child.

Money vs. Finance

Further blurring the lines between financial myth and reality, we now live in a time when money is rarely seen and understood even by adults. We've progressed to a culture of finance. It's utterly important that your teen understand the difference.

Gone are the days of paying for everything with cash. If you ever carry a $50 or $100 bill with you, you'll start to notice how many stores won't even accept them due to counterfeit concerns. It's as if our society frowns upon using cash in lieu of debit and credit cards. The tangibility of dollars has been exchanged for plastic, whether punching a few numbers for our purchase or simply signing a piece of paper. How are the children of today ever to understand there was a time when "cash was king"?

In its simplest terms, money is something you carry in your pocket. You might use it to pay for your groceries or for a lunch out this week. It's tangible and simple to comprehend and work with. The world of finance, however, seems more vague and less tangible. Consider the purchasing of a home. Perhaps you've done so recently or are on your way to doing so. How much would you pay for your home, $80,000, $340,000, or $800,000? Even if your home were on the low side of $80,000 (if this price even exists in most major cities), try going to your local bank and requesting this amount of money in cash for your purchase. It just doesn't happen any more.

I remember one of my bank managers telling me that when he started, many years ago, all bank managers were equipped with guns and it was common for them to help out if a competing bank ran short on money. He told me that he would simply load up his briefcase with as much as half a million dollars in cash and deliver it to the bank in need himself. In today's world, for so many obvious reasons, solid security companies are now equipped with guns and other means for transporting cash safely and securely.

Large amounts of money are rarely handled today. This is true whether you're a bank manager or a consumer ready to purchase a big-ticket item. We live in an age of finance. Whatever amount you decide to spend on your home, you will likely just be signing pieces of paper. Could you imagine transporting the hundreds of thousands of dollars to the person selling the home to you? I'm not sure the seller would even take your money considering the number of counterfeit bills out there now.

The larger the purchase, the more slips of paper you end up signing. What's the point? We must first understand the difference between money in our hand and finance—the pieces of paper that signify a promise to repay the value of our big-ticket item. As with lending, many investors will also sign and receive regular pieces of paper when investing their money. Gone are the days portrayed in movies when you could roll around in your money. Many stocks won't even directly issue you a certificate when purchasing their shares. If they do, it's usually held with a broker or mutual fund company. Many adults don't ever really feel their assets or debts anymore.

Let's try a game that will hopefully bring back the feeling of money's tangibility. Try it on your own first and then introduce it to your child. You may wish to use a lesser dollar amount with your child, depending upon what they're used to seeing as a cash amount in your household. This is a powerful yet simple game by Fredric Lehrman from his audio program *Prosperity Consciousness*.

Imagine for a moment that I've given you $1,000 to play this game. You only need a couple of minutes of uninterrupted time to play, so find a quiet spot for a few moments. The rules for the game and spending the money are as follows:

- You must spend the entire $1,000 on yourself.
- You must spend the money for your own pleasure and to be enjoyed within that day, not some future time period.
- You are not allowed to make a payment for something you'll realize in the future, pay a bill, or give to charity.

Remember, this is just a game to see what you'd spend the money on for your own pleasure within a 24-hour period.

Are you ready? Now write down what ideas first come to mind:

1. _____
2. _____
3. _____
4. _____
5. _____

Were you able to spend the $1,000 quite effortlessly? Did you spend it within a day? Great! Congratulations. You've won today's game.

Let's play again. Same rules, same dollar amount. Take a few moments to detail what you would purchase the next day and it must be something different than the first.

1. _____
2. _____
3. _____
4. _____
5. _____

Were you successful again? I imagine this task was still relatively effortless. Now fast forward to day three, and four, and even seven. Take a few minutes to think of new ways and items that you might purchase for your own pleasure for each of those days. How about every day for thirty days? What about every day for an entire year? How do you feel about this game now?

Whenever I play this fun game during my lectures, I find, as you might have, that most participants start running out of ideas by about day seven. I have yet to experience an audience that could easily make it to week two and certainly they are much slower at coming up with ideas by then. Participants report that the game isn't fun after the first week and spending the money becomes a chore, an effort.

Spending a mere $1,000 per day is not a difficult task. After all, $1,000 per day is just $365,000 per year, which really isn't an astronomical amount of money. There are a good number of people who earn more than that as an annual salary. I know of friends and clients who spend more than this on average in a year and they still manage to go about their lives without the "spending of this money" becoming an all-consuming task. With the advent of the Internet, I could easily spend $1,000 per day for my own pleasure by the time I've finished my morning coffee, and for many years, before

I would ever run out of ideas, if I ever did.

So what's the purpose of the game? It's threefold. First, by chunking down an amount that most of us can relate to, we can picture what we might purchase with that money. It's likely that if you've traveled recently, you carried that much cash (if not more) on your holiday. It's a tangible amount and can be spent easily within a day or week. I want you to feel what spending that amount means to you as we so rarely use cash in our society any more and have moved into the nebulous world of finance—just trading and signing pieces of paper.

Second, if you had difficulty spending the imaginary money past the first week or month, you might have a problem with money: should you amass your ideal fortune, you might not reap the benefits and luxuries that money can provide. By not consciously knowing what you would do with the $1,000 past day ten, for example, you could at some level be saying, "No, no, don't give me the money yet (which could be a raise in salary, increased sales, etc.), I don't even know what to do with it."

Our aim here is for total congruency about receiving money in our lives and reaping the pleasures that it affords us. Furthermore, if you couldn't come up with a reasonable amount of items for your spending pleasure, what's the point of pursing more wealth? By revisiting this game and playing until you can comfortably come up with several months of spending with little to no effort, you're affirming to your subconscious that you deserve and are comfortable with spending money on yourself and for your own pleasure.

The third and last point to this game is to identify how much wealth you really need to feel financially secure. Over the years, when I've asked clients or participants at lectures how much they need in a bank account to feel financially set, the majority in my informal polling come up with unrealistic numbers. Some state dollar amounts such as several millions when they might be only earning five-figure incomes. When asked to play the game, if they could barely make it past week one, spending this relatively small amount of money (compared to their goals of having several million dollars), why would they feel they needed so much? You might also want to re-examine your financial "comfort" goal. Do you still need as much as you thought, or could your goal be adjusted to a more realistic amount after playing this game?

Try playing this game annually with your child. Encourage them to have a list of dozens if not hundreds of items, products and services that they would like to spend their money on for their own personal pleasure. Each year, have your child create a new list and look back at the old one to see if any of their previous years' desires were actualized. Depending on how much cash your child and your family are used to dealing with, you may wish to reduce this amount.

Advanced Goal Setting and Manifestation

The Six-Degrees Game
As an advocate of our ability to manifest the power of attraction, intention, and focus, I was amazed at the impact a recent television show had on my belief in what is known as the six-degrees theory. The basic premise is that within about six people or "degrees," one can be connected through their own social network to just about anyone on the planet. In December 2006, I happened upon an ABC Primetime show experimenting with the six-degrees notion. I only caught the second part of the program, but it was truly fascinating.

The interviewer was visiting Pete, a twenty-something African American boxer from the "projects." Pete's challenge was to locate a particular dancer on Broadway, who just received a role in the famous musical *A Chorus Line*. Pete was shown a picture of the lovely young lady and the challenge was presented. He needed to locate the performer in six steps or less by using his own network of people. He wasn't allowed to research the dancer and try to make contact by seeking her out via yellow pages, the Internet, or other such means.

When asked if Pete thought he'd be successful, he shook his head quickly back and forth and proclaimed it wasn't likely at all. When the interviewer inquired further, Pete said he and the dancer were from different worlds. He didn't know anyone in the arts and as a boxer raised in the projects, he didn't feel there was any way it could be done.

During the first part of the show, one very wealthy and prestigious businesswoman and a successful businessman were to find Pete using the same method as Pete had been asked to find the dancer. They had been successful in finding him. When it was Pete's turn, he pointed out that he thought it was much easier for the wealthy to find someone in the projects. He said it would be easier for someone looking down to find someone at the bottom, but when you're at the bottom looking up, it's much more difficult. Apparently, Pete felt this dancer was quite a bit "above" him.

Though predicting defeat, Pete did accept the challenge. The first person he called was a woman he grew up with in the projects. Her family had moved on when they were kids, but they had always kept in touch and he considered her his sister. She was a stylish and attractive young woman who worked at an extremely posh store in Manhattan. Pete called his "sister," wondering if she would assist him on his challenge. She told Pete that there was a very influential gentleman in the store at the time of his call and perhaps this fellow could point them in the right direction. We'll call him degree number two; the sister was degree number one.

The ABC interviewer and Pete arrived at the store in a stretched limo with cameras in tow. It wasn't difficult to get Pete's longtime friend to help him along. The arts fellow knew of a dancer on the other side of town who might be somehow linked to the dancer they were looking for. We'll call her degree number three. This woman was a bartender during the day, so they headed over to the pub she worked at. Sure enough, degree number three had heard the name of the dancer they were looking for. She didn't know her personally, but did know the studio where she danced. She referred them to the woman that heads the dance studio. Degree number four.

Sure enough, they headed to the dance studio and the head of the establishment proclaimed that the dancer they sought was just there practicing that morning. She made a few phone calls for Pete and found out the Broadway theatre the dancer was practicing at.

They headed to this theatre next to introduce Pete and the dancer. It was amazing to see Pete and his reaction to the success of the exercise. It seemed that little effort and even time was required for him to come face to face with the woman he was to find. Armed with simply her name, trying to reach her via the phone book, Internet, or other means may not have produced as efficient a system. And the dancer, being in on the game, was delighted when Pete finally found her proclaiming that she knew he would.

So what is it about six degrees? Scientists who have studied this theory claim that anyone, within approximately six degrees, could locate almost anyone else, using a human chain, or network, to do so. The "small world phenomenon" (also known as the "small world effect") is the hypothesis that everyone in the world can be reached through a short chain of social acquaintances. The concept gave rise to the famous phrase "six degrees of separation" after a 1967 small-world experiment by social psychologist Stanley Milgram, which suggested that two random U.S. citizens were connected on average by a chain of six acquaintances.

Imagine what a profound effect the practice of this theory could have on your teen's life. Imagine how your own life could be altered if you truly believed that you could meet almost anyone you desired just by using a few of your contacts as a chain to link you to the person you'd like to meet or know.

I'm sure your teen is familiar with Kevin Bacon and the famous *Six Degrees of Kevin Bacon* game. Given this example and that of the ABC Primetime show, this should be enough to convince your teen to give it a try as an experiment of curiosity and perhaps of concrete benefit. I'm personally giving this game a try and will outline my goals and process. I will then sketch out one you might use with your child, and possibly for yourself as well.

I've been lucky enough to meet two of my heroes in life: Dr. Deepak Chopra and Dr. Wayne Dyer. I met Dr. Chopra in a way that anyone could have and many did. I purchased a ticket to a presentation of his when he was in my city. I also bought one of his books and waited in line for an hour to have a 20-second chat with him while he autographed it.

Meeting Dr. Dyer was more of a chance encounter and a "had to be in the right place at the right time" kind of coincidence. It was at a company conference just a couple of hours before I was to check out and head home. A series of seemingly insignificant events would place me steps away from one of my heroes. It was only because I knew Dr. Dyer's voice from listening to his audio programs for many years that I recognized his voice from behind an enormous centrepiece as he chatted on his cell phone. This encounter lasted many more moments than that of Dr. Chopra's and I had the unique experience of being the only fan present at the time to receive 100% of Dr. Dyer's time and attention.

A new hero whom I've added to my list is Oprah Winfrey. I admire her greatly, and as an author writing primarily on the psychology of money, I think Oprah is as well rounded as a person gets. She's exceedingly wealthy and seems to enjoy, spend, and donate her money freely. And as a wannabe journalist, I imagine that she'd be a fantastic person to interview on the topics of success and rising above adversity.

Shortly after watching ABC's Primetime show on the six-degrees concept, I decided to give the game a try of my own. I've enlisted the support of ten individuals who will provide ten human chains in my quest to meet Oprah. You might be thinking, "Why don't you, your staff, or your publisher just ring her up yourselves?" Good question. But as you might imagine, Oprah has quite the team of gatekeepers and there's even books written on the subject of getting on her show. It's not quite as simple as my publicist just calling her up requesting an interview. And as an author, and for my publisher, there's no greater and quicker success than being on Oprah's show. An obvious benefit is selling books, but, more important, I'd just love to meet her, have a few minutes of her time, and interview her successful attitudes and share them with other readers.

On to my experiment. I have e-mailed hundreds of contacts and have short-listed the participants to ten. The idea is that each of my volunteers will try out the six-degrees concept on my behalf with the end result hopefully allowing me to meet and interview Oprah.

My enticement for my participants and those they employ for assistance in getting to Oprah is to give them the gift of one of my books. Also, in exchange for their time and to ensure that my ten trails don't run cold, I will also offer the option of reciprocity. I will help each of my ten volunteers try and locate their hero or person they'd like to meet via the small-world theory should they wish to take me up on it.

Will it work? I haven't a clue. I suspect it will and know that it will be tremendous fun experimenting with the process. If you'd like to follow my human chains and their progress, visit my website at www.theproperityfactor.com. Whether or not we're successful with this experiment, I'm sure they'll be plenty of side benefits for all involved, independent of my desire to meet Oprah Winfrey.

Your Child's Six-Degrees Game

One must keep in mind that ABC Primetime had the benefit of using cameras and fame to entice their guests to play along. To paraphrase Andy Warhol, everyone will have their fifteen minutes of fame. As such, cameras are enough of an inducement to play along, but what about your child and the rest of us? How do we keep the chain moving? Below are some tips that will help your child get started:

- People, including teens, really do like to be asked for help. Being trusted and needed is often enough to entice others to assist your child on their anticipated path.
- Should your child need further weight beyond the pledge of willingness from others, how about a simple offer of reciprocity? Encourage your teen to offer the same support to those they're enlisting.
- Your teen's contact list likely isn't as large as mine, so before starting, assist them in identifying individuals whom either of you know. Also, unlike my experiment, they don't need ten chains to get started. One

chain will do and that simply starts with identifying one individual who will help them on their way.

- Monitor the trail. With my example, part of the reason for offering a book to each participant is that I must be sent their mailing address to do so. As each person in my chain introduces the next, they need to e-mail me, thereby creating a measurable path for me. With your child's experiment, consider having them set up a blog, which are available for free on the Internet. As contacts are made, each person can write a quick post of their progress. Alternatively, requesting that each person e-mail your child will work well too.
- Who should your teen try to meet? I recommend that it can literally be anyone, but I do suggest staying away from celebrities and sports personalities. Your teen is welcome to strive, but high-profile individuals may be much more difficult for the first experiment. What career aspirations does your teen have? Perhaps identifying successful individuals aligned with their career goals would be a good place to start. What about a politician, journalist, author, successful CEO, or local artist?

A word of caution: You should play this game with your teen each step of the way and monitor progress and successes together. Unfortunately, we live in a day and age where predators lurk on the Internet and in other locations. If someone along the chain is requesting to meet or talk with your teen, it would be best to be there with them. A successful completion of this exercise may be to meet with the person they've focused on. Although your child may idolize this individual, it's still utterly important that they have adult supervision during this process.

• Encourage your child to grasp the concept that they really are able to connect with other humans who they might feel are outside of their reach. You needn't play this game at all if your child is unwilling. You both could instead simply make direct contact with those they'd like to meet. Certainly, the six-degrees game is worth exploring, but your child will also enjoy a rich experience trying to connect with others directly. The choice is yours.

When I was just starting out in the financial industry, a fellow brought in from our head office in England had a great strategy that I was willing to try. He suggested "mirroring" and learning from local successful businesspeople just for the experience—not to sell them anything, just to interview them to elicit what made them successful. I attempted this exercise by dusting off my local chamber of commerce directory and chose a number of business leaders whom I had recognized from being profiled in the media. As instructed, I developed a non-sales letter asking for fifteen minutes of their time and that as a young person just starting out in the financial industry, I just wanted to know what made them successful.

With great anticipation and trepidation, I called the few dozen successful people who received my introductory letters. As a young adult, I was thrilled at the number of appointments I was able to arrange. After meeting with a number of individuals (all of who, interestingly enough, stated that they really didn't consider themselves successful), I was pleasantly surprised at their willingness to share their stories. They were eager to help me with my goals even though I hadn't asked them to. The path that I then set upon after meeting with these successful people has certainly shaped my life and likely determined much of my aspirations, opportunities, and future journeys.

It wasn't just the interviews that were important, it was also the ancillary benefits that made this experiment so interesting. Some fourteen years later, I'm able to look back and see how so many small steps ultimately led to large accomplishments. As an adult, you've likely perfected your hindsight view as well. Although many teenagers might have a hard time hearing your life analysis and appreciating your words of wisdom, sharing them with your child will be helpful nonetheless.

Strategic By-Products

On a recent plane ride to Denver for a book tour stop, I had the pleasure of meeting a brilliant and articulate businessperson by the name of Grant Ericksen. Grant was to have a seat a few aisles back, but a family wanting their children to sit near each other asked Grant if he would move. He did and landed next to me. After a nap and skimming the newspaper, Grant and I struck up a conversation.

It was forty-five minutes or so before we had even introduced ourselves. I didn't know that this was one of the most successful car dealers in my city sitting right next to me. What fascinated me most about him was a question that he had asked me early in our conversation. "What brings you delight?" he inquired. I really had to think about that one. *Delight* isn't a word I often use in my vocabulary. As I inquired further, Grant shared that he has a "delight book," where he records events and occurrences, large and small, that bring delight to his life. He also has his children ask that question of themselves. For Grant, it's much more than material success and money that make him and his family happy and that was evident by his early questioning. Instead of asking only about what I did for a living, my background, my income, or my successes, Grant

184 — Kelley Keehn

was most interested in what I found delight in.

Another "Ericksenism" is his theory of strategic bi-products. He explained that it's often what comes across our path as we're on our journey to a goal that is worth more than the attainment of the goal itself. A salesperson might wake up tomorrow with winning over his customers that day as his only goal. He may or may not be successful, but perhaps he, unbeknownst to him, will meet the woman he will one day marry and eventually have many children with. The bi-product for me that day was when a family asked Grant to move next to me, giving us the opportunity for an enriching conversation—and to think that I was focused merely on getting to Denver.

When you explain the six-degrees game and decide to play with your teen, explain the strategic bi-product notion as well. Your child's desired meeting is important indeed, but it's more vital that they recognize the benefits that affect them and others along the way.

To help your teen understand that life's successes are often found on the journey, consider these examples:

• Your child tries out for the high-school football team and meets a cheerleader that will one day be his wife.
• Your child suffers a minor injury while skiing and she loses her star title on the soccer team. Shifting her focus to perfecting her skill at playing the piano, years later she is invited to play for your city's symphony.
• Your child flies halfway across the country to try his signing talent for the show *American Idol* and is abysmally unsuccessful. However, his charisma and animated antics are seen on television by one of America's top acting scouts and he's groomed into a successful actor.

Chances of success aside, it's the side benefits that some-times make all the difference. Can you and your teen think of at least five outcomes presently or in the past where a strate-gic bi-product may have been overlooked or should be cel-ebrated?

1. _____
2. _____
3. _____
4. _____
5. _____

I'd like to assist you and your child should you decide to tackle the six-degrees experiment. E-mail me at info@ theprosperityfactor.com and share your successes, struggles, and strategic bi-products. I'd also be thrilled to enlist the sup-port of other readers, so let me know if you'd like your ques-tions and comments to remain anonymous or if you'd like me to share them with everyone for global support to this im-portant experience.

Your Child's Prosperity Action Steps

- Have you set up the credit account with your child and outlined clear goals, penalties, guidelines, and re-payment schedules? Have you determined a per-centage split for your child's income into the long-term savings account, targeted savings ac-count, and piggy bank, while also factoring in repay-ment of their credit?

- Have you set spending dates with your child and checked in with them about their spending habits, both positive and negative?

- Have you explained credit reports to your child and pre-ventative measures for keeping their credit in good standing? Have you checked your own credit report, especially in a day and age with so much credit fraud?

- Did you and your child try the $1,000 game? How many days were you each able to play for? Could you e-mail friends and family and explain the game and elicit their spending thoughts if yours couldn't extend past day thirty?

- Have you tried the six-degrees game with your child? Do you need help with it? If so, please e-mail me at info@theprosperityfactor.com and visit my website www.theprosperityfactor.com for tips from other readers and to share your own.

- What strategic bi-products have you and your child identified? Please chart your child's progress carefully and if they aren't initially successful with specific goals, help them identify important lessons and other benefits received along the way. Remember, it's not the end but the journey that's the most important. Evaluate the "path" when possible as opposed to just how close your child is from achieving their goals.

Afterword

It's often said by authors that if a reader learns or applies one concept found in a book, the book is a success. I've made an effort to offer you and your child much more than a single concept. My heartfelt hope is that I've been successful. I want the both of you to have a healthy relationship with money. To feel good about finances, we don't have to be experts, but it is essential that your child is empowered to assimilate the often complicated world of money management.

As artist Nathaniel Emmons declared, "Habit is either the best of servants or the worst of masters." To fully experience *The Prosperity Factor for Kids*, completing (or, at the very minimum, trying) the exercises with your child will help you both create new and prosperous habits and beliefs. These in turn will form powerful actions that, when consistently undertaken, will transform your lives in miraculous ways.

I myself used to skip over the lessons and exercises of various types, promising myself that I'd get back to them "one day" and would assume that it's simply enough to just think of them. I can assure you that your child will miss the benefits and the entire purpose of this program if they do the same.

If you need the assistance of a fellow parent or support group to help you and your child motivate one another to finish the exercises, consider starting one today and visit my website for a complete kit to starting your own book club or prosperity group. Not only will teaching the material instill it deeper within your subconscious and that of your child's but you'll also create accountability by completing the exercises with others on a like mission. Please e-mail me and visit my website for a number of free exercises and a question-and-answer forum where I will post answers to all readers' questions.

I've also included a convenient checklist at the end of the book so you can quickly review the exercises and ensure that you and your child haven't missed any. Use this easy reference guide as an annual tradition with your child or during your family money meetings. Find a new journal or goal book for your child each year and make special appointments with them to review last year's progress and to celebrate achievements.

Although we've never met, your child's successes, struggles, and triumphs are important to me. I'm grateful that you've taken the time to offer me the opportunity to share parts of my life, philosophy, and teachings with you. It has been my honor and privilege, and I truly wish you and your family much success and happiness.

Most of all, it is my wish that your child achieves all that they desire and that they always remember that they are a unique and special individual. I also want them to realize they deserve all that their heart desires and that they are already superstars and valuable human beings, independent of their future financial successes.

I hope you've enjoyed the journey to your child's prosperity factor. Start tapping into the miracles and tools that are available to you and your child. May God bless you and your family on your journey. I hope to meet you there one day.

Live prosperously!

Kelley

Your Prosperity Action Steps Checklist

Check each item that you and your child have completed. If you haven't finished an item, indicate your estimated date of achievement.

Section I—Ages Two to Five

❏ Have you taken the time to complete the self-assessment questionnaire? Did you reveal any "lack of money" issues that you hadn't thought of before?

❏ Have you taken time to develop positive money memories with your child?

❏ Have you purchased a formal piggy bank for your child?

❏ Have you obtained and examined foreign currencies with your child? What hidden messages did you locate within the $1 bill that you hadn't noticed before?

❏ Have you carefully examined and identified potentially harmful words and statements regarding money and wealth that you will no longer use?

❏ Have you set up a regular spending date with your child even if it's only once a month? Does your child have a schedule of upcoming spending dates to look forward to?

❏ Have you thought of any excesses in your life and that of your child's that could be used to give to others?

Section II—Ages Six to Ten

❏ Have you set up the targeted savings account with your child and outlined clear goals and timelines? Did you determine a percentage split for your child's income into this account and their piggy bank?

❏ What motivational style best suits your child? Have you experimented with both to determine which works best and when?

❏ Have you determined and discussed a household chore schedule for your child? Have you clearly outlined a dollar amount that you are willing to pay them for an allowance or remuneration for household duties?

❏ Have you set a schedule for your family money meetings? Have you determined how often you will hold them and where?

❏ Have you taken a few moments to introduce your child to various acts of kindness? Did you think of more together?

Section III—Ages Eleven to Fifteen

❏ Have you set up the long-term savings account with your child and outlined clear goals and timelines? Did you determine a percentage split for your child's income into this account, the targeted savings account, and their piggy bank? Did you decide with your child whether to change their piggy bank's name to the "pleasure account"?

❏ Have you tried any money-seeking activities with your child yet? Did you attempt the anti-budget game?

❏ Have you tried to locate additional sources of income or create new sources with your child? Did you try the economy game? Did you contact your child's school to garner their support? What about the willingness of your child's friends and family to play along?

❏ Have you taken the time to watch the film *National Treasure* with your child and to define what money, wealth, and prosperity means to your family?

❏ Have you taken the time to watch the film *Pay It Forward* with your child? Did you try any random acts of kindness together?

❏ Have you tried the 30-Day Challenge and are you still wearing your bracelets? Are you and your child focusing more on what you want as opposed to what you don't?

❏ Have you spent time with your child to identify their goals?

Section IV—Ages Sixteen to Eighteen

❑ Have you set up the credit account with your child and outlined clear goals, penalties, guidelines, and repayment schedules? Have you and your child determined a percentage split for your child's income into the long-term savings account, the targeted savings account, and the piggy bank, while also factoring in repayment of their credit?

❑ Have you set predetermined spending dates with your child and checked in with them about their spending habits, both positive and negative?

❑ Have you explained credit reports to your child and preventative measures for keeping their credit in good standing? Have your checked your own credit report, especially in a day and age of so much credit fraud?

❑ Have you both tried the $1,000 game? If you or your child had problems coming up with items past thirty days, did you e-mail friends and family, explain the game to them, and then elicit their spending thoughts?

❑ Have you tried the six-degrees game with your child? Did you e-mail me if you needed further help from me or other readers?

❑ Have you identified a number of strategic by-products with your child? Did you chart your progress and focus on the journey as opposed to just the end goal?

Notes

1. Gresham's law. Answers.com. Dictionary of Finance and Investment Terms, Barron's Educational Series, Inc, 2006. http://www.answers.com/topic/gresham-s-law, accessed February 21, 2007.
2. Jessica Bennett, "Spend Cycle," *Newsweek*, August, 8, 2006.
3. credit card. Answers.com. Encyclopedia of American History, Answers Corporation, 2006. http://www.answers.com/topic/charge-card, accessed February 21, 2007.

Resources

Financial Resources for Families In Need

The following is a partial list and explanation of state resources for children and their care. You'll find a link for a complete and up-to-date list along with full explanations on my website at www.theprosperityfactor.com:

Arizona Cash Assistance Program. This program provides temporary cash assistance and supportive services to children, individuals, and their families.

CalWORKs/TANF. This is a welfare program that gives cash aid and services to eligible needy California families. The program serves all fifty-eight counties in the state and is operated locally by county welfare departments.

Chafee Foster Care Independence Program. This program assists states and localities in establishing and carrying out programs designed to assist foster youth likely to remain in foster care until eighteen years of age.

Child Care Access. This program supports the participation of low-income parents in post-secondary education through the provision of campus-based childcare services.

Child Care Resource and Referral Services. These services help parents locate and choose quality childcare by providing referrals to local child care providers, information on state licensing requirements, and the availability of childcare subsidies.

Child Support Enforcement (CSE). This program provides services to locate absent parents, establish paternity, and enforce support obligations.

Child Tax Credit. This program can reduce the Federal tax you owe by $1,000 for each qualifying child under the age of seventeen.

Child and Dependent Care Credit. This program can reduce your tax by claiming the credit for child and dependent care expenses on your federal income-tax return.

Foster Care. This program provides federal financial assistance to states to assist with:

1) Costs of foster care maintenance for eligible children.

2) Administrative costs to manage the program.

3) Training for staff, foster parents, and private agency staff.

Immunization Grants. The Vaccines for Children (VFC) program purchases vaccines for children in certain eligibility groups who can't afford to buy vaccines. Doctors can get these vaccines for their patients who qualify by joining the VFC program in their state.

Indian Child Welfare Act Title II Grants. The purpose of this program is to promote the stability and security of American Indian/Alaskan Native families by protecting their children and preventing the separation of their families.

Indiana Temporary Assistance for Needy Families (TANF). This program is designed to help welfare recipients obtain and maintain jobs. This program provides assistance to families with children and requires adults to work or prepare for work.

Iowa Family Investment Program (TANF). The Family Investment Program (FIP) is Iowa's Temporary Assistance to Needy Families (TANF) program. FIP provides cash assistance to needy families, as they become self-supporting so children may be cared for in their own homes or in the homes of relatives.

Kentucky Transitional Assistance Program (K-TAP). This is

the monetary assistance program established by Kentucky using federal funds from the TANF block grant. K-TAP provides financial and medical assistance.

Medical Dental Expenses Tax Credit. This program can reduce the federal tax you owe by medical expense deductions.

Michigan Family Independence Program. The Family Independence Program (FIP) provides cash assistance to families with children and pregnant women to help them pay for living expenses such as rent, heat, utilities, clothing, food, and personal care items.

Michigan Food Assistance Program. This program supplements the food purchasing power of low-income individuals and families. The U.S. Department of Agriculture funds 100% of this program. The state and federal governments share administrative costs.

North Dakota Temporary Assistance for Needy Families (TANF). This program provides funds to assist families in any manner that is reasonable. These include: assisting needy families to care for children in their homes; reducing dependency of needy parents by promoting job preparation, work, and marriage; preventing out-of-wedlock pregnancies; and encouraging the formation and maintenance of two-parent families.

Oregon Temporary Assistance for Needy Families. This program provides cash assistance to low income families with children while they strive to become self-sufficient.

Pennsylvania Temporary Assistance for Needy Families (TANF). Temporary Assistance for Needy Families (TANF) provides money for dependent children and their parents or other relatives with whom they live, and for pregnant women.

Social Services Block Grant (SSBG). This is a capped entitlement program that provides funds to assist states in delivering social services directed toward the needs of children and adults.

South Dakota Temporary Assistance for Needy Families (TANF). This is a temporary public assistance program administered by the South Dakota Department of Social Services and Department of Labor.

Special Improvement Project. The purpose of this grant is to provide funding for projects that further the national child support mission and goals.

Tax Benefits for Adoption. This program enables individuals to take a tax credit of up to $10,000 for qualifying expenses paid to adopt an eligible child (including a child with special needs).

Tax Benefits for Education. This program offers a tax reduction through an education credit.

Source: www.govbenefits.gov

Resources for Student Aid

Federal Student Aid. A source for free information from the U.S. Department of Education on preparing for and funding education beyond hight school. www.studentaid.ed.gov

The Department of Veterans Affairs (VA). Offers several programs administered by its Education Service. Aid is available for veterans, reservists, National Guard persons, widows, and orphans.

Disabled American Veterans. In memory of the late Secretary of Veterans Affairs, Jesse Brown, the Disabled American Veterans has established the Jesse Brown Memorial Youth Scholarship Program.

The United States Army. Offers education benefits for individuals enlisting in selected military occupational specialties. The Montgomery GI Bill and the Army's College Fund offer financial assistance to pay for future education expenses. Students leaving college may be eligible for the Army's Loan Repayment Program. This enlistment option, for active Army or Army Reserve, repays eligible federally insured loans for education.

AmeriCorps. Administered by the Corporation for National and Community Service, AmeriCorps allows people of all ages and backgrounds to earn educational awards in exchange for a year of community service.

The Department of Health and Human Services. Offers scholarships and loan repayment programs through its Indian Health Service and National Institutes of Health (NIH).

The Department of Labor. Here you will find a variety of useful information, from how to further your education to suggestions to help you with your child's job search. www.careervoyages.org

students.gov. Provides links to scholarship and grant sites, state aid information, and more.

studentjobs.gov. Developed as a partnership between the U.S.Office of Personnel Management and government agencies, this website is similar to students.gov but focuses on employment. But, while you're at the site, be sure to click on "e-Scholar" for numerous sources of federal scholarships, internships fellowships, etc.

Resources for Canadian Readers

This book has been specifically updated to reflect an American reader. If you are Canadian or moving to Canada, please visit www.theprosperityfactor.com for a complete list of Canadian-specific governement benefits, education savings programs, tax benefits, and more.

Index

Acknowledgements

After many years of lecturing and writing on the subject of "foundational" financial concepts and listening to the feedback of those who read *The Prosperity Factor* and *The Woman's Guide to Money*, I am privileged to have had the opportunity to again put my ideas and concepts into written form.

It's been said that it takes a village to raise a child, but I think it takes a city to support an author. This book, as with any life project, would have never happened without the encouragement, assistance, and love I received from so many people.

First, to the readers of *The Prosperity Factor* and *The Woman's Guide to Money*, I extend my heartfelt thanks. The greatest part about being a writer is hearing from my readers. For those of you who took the time to share your comments and courageous stories in letters and e-mails, I am grateful. Each one of you brings delight to my life.

To my incredible mother, Kathleen. If there are angels that walk among us, you're one of them. Thank you for your wisdom, love, and efforts in helping me finish this book (and the other three) and for cheering me along every step of the way. Thank you for being the greatest financial teacher I have had the honor of knowing. I'm so proud of you, Mom! As Abraham Lincoln so eloquently stated, "All that I am, all that I've been, and all that I'll ever be, I owe to my mother."

To my love and greatest business coach on the planet, Wyatt Cavanaugh. I thank you for believing in me always, especially when I didn't believe in myself. Thank you for instilling the challenging yet positive thought that I could and should write a book and for sticking with me through this fourth one. My eternal gratitude for your numerous insights, support, and daily back massages.

To my amazing family, without whom I never would have had the courage to start this project or any other. When you have a family and support system like I have been blessed with, it makes writing about abundance and prosperity a relatively easy task. My gratitude to my brother David for his lifelong intellectual debates and his love and support, without which I wouldn't have grown as much as a human and spiritual being. To my brother Randy and his wife, Elaine, and my beautiful nieces, Amelia, Alyshia, Jocelyn, and my little buddy Adam. I hope to have a family as marvellous as yours one day. And to my father, Edward, for teaching me to think and for instilling a lifelong love of learning.

Without the support of my remarkable publisher Insomniac Press, this material may have never been considered. To my patient and encouraging publisher, Mike O'Connor. To be sure, it is the thrill of any writer to complete a book, but it's a great honor to have someone who believes in your work enough to publish it. And to my very tolerant and talented editor, Dan Varrette. I thank you for making sense out of my material and for your unyielding style for creating quality work and making your author appear competent.

To my business editor at the *Edmonton Sun*, Tim LeRiche. If I've improved as a writer at all, and I'm not sure that I have, I owe you a debt of gratitude for your time, patience, and care in grooming me to be the journalist I hope to be one day.

An enormous thank you goes out to the team at CTV Edmonton for allowing me to test this material with you and your viewers each month. I'd especially like to thank Jeanette Osadchuk, Carrie Doll, Daryl MacIntyre, Maria Orydzuk, Brian Marshall, Ken Mitchell, Sylvia Osadchuk, and Maggie Thomas.

I would like to extend my gratitude to RBC Financial Group for granting me permission to use their "Giving the Gift of Knowledge" RESP guide for section one of this book. Namely, my sincere thanks goes to Kathy Bevan for her support and getting this information approved with laser speed.

To all of my close and superb friends, family, and supporters of this book and *The Woman's Guide to Money* who have listened to me talk about this book, supported me emotionally throughout the process, and offered their assistance and ideas freely. To list each of you individually would no doubt take more pages than that of this book. Know that your love and cheerleading along the way never ceases to amaze and bless me.

In saving the best for last, my heartfelt thanks to my creator, God, for allowing me to be born in a time and country that embraces equality, freedom, and opportunity for all who seek it. I am truly blessed!

About the Author

Kelley Keehn, EPC, is a financial expert, author, speaker, coach, radio host, columnist, and corporate trainer. She is the author of *The Woman's Guide to Money*, *The Prosperity Factor*, and the co-author of *Mutual Fundamentals II*.

As a former financial professional of over a decade, Kelley's witnessed first hand the problems individuals have with money. Early in her career, she began to study the underlying principles of the wealthy. Her continuous research was first taught in her stunningly effective Prosperity Factor courses. Since then, these principles and strategies have been captured and published in *The Prosperity Factor* and *The Woman's Guide to Money*; both being practical guides to making changes to the way we think of money at a fundamental level.

At the age of twenty-one, Kelley was already overseeing hundreds of millions of dollars in assets for one of Canada's international banks. Her innovative training programs and strategies were taught to branch staff at not one but two major Canadian financial institutions. Wanting more, Kelley opened Keehn Financial in the year 2000 and sold her firm in 2005.

Kelley is a regular columnist with Sun Media, the *Edmonton Sun*, *Canadian MoneySaver* magazine, *Orb* magazine, *Husband and Wife* magazine, and was a daily guest on California 103 FM radio, is a monthly guest with CTV Edmonton, and is a regular guest on television and radio shows around the globe.

Kelley travels extensively throughout North America as a faculty member with the Canadian and American Initiative for Elder Planning Studies, as a sought-after corporate lecturer, and for her book tours. Kelley also serves as a faculty member for CIEPS and a keynote and seminar presenter for some of the most world-renowned financial institutions.

Kelley resides in Edmonton, Alberta, Canada, with Wyatt and their pampered four-legged friends, Thoreau, Voltaire, Oscar, and Mr. Howls.

For a complete background on Kelley and where to find her, visit www.kelleykeehn.com.

Made in the USA